Richer Than A Millionaire

Richer Than A Millionaire

A Pathway to True Prosperity

William D. Danko and Richard J. Van Ness

ISBN-13: 9780692912713
ISBN-10: 0692912711

To Anthony J. Danko (1947–2015)—
in all ways spiritual, Tony was
far richer than a millionaire.

Contents

LIST OF TABLES AND FIGURES

ACKNOWLEDGMENTS

In 1973, I took a marketing class given by Professor Tom Stanley. Shortly thereafter, I assisted him with his first study of the affluent market. Over the next twenty years, we collaborated on many research projects about wealth in America, culminating with our 1996 book *The Millionaire Next Door*. These experiences inspired the current project.

While I enjoyed a rich career in academia and on the speaking circuit, I was always drawn to what is really important: family. I have been blessed with my loving wife, Connie, and my children—Christy (Ben), Todd (Karen), and David—as well as five precious grandchildren: Eva, Walter, Charlie, Hazel, and Violet. All of these loved ones have made me far richer than a millionaire.

I would be remiss if I did not mention the many colleagues, especially Sal Belardo, Bill Holstein, Hugh Farley, and Don Bourque, who provide me with important guidance on a regular basis.

As I reflect on my career with my colleague Rich Van Ness, we hope to share our cumulative insights about true wealth.

William D. Danko, PhD

Acknowledgments

I thank my colleague Bill Danko for welcoming me aboard for the research mission of finding what is truly needed to be richer than a millionaire.

We are grateful for the entrepreneurship research findings provided by my brother, Raymond K. Van Ness, PhD. We thank our colleague Edith (Edie) M. Donohue, PhD, who contributed vignettes that are based on cases from her career in employment transition services. Many thanks to my wife, Mary, who provided continuous encouragement and vital assistance whenever requested. Thanks to my entire family for the realization of true prosperity!

Richard J. Van Ness, PhD

INTRODUCTION

R ich Van Ness and Bill Danko have worked with each other on various projects over the past thirty years. One recurring discussion centers on the lessons we hope to pass down to our children and grandchildren, especially given our roles as educators to thousands of students during our teaching careers.

It is clear to us that many young people are clueless about their direction in life. Yes, they want a career, and yes, they want a good life, but knowing what to do is to many quite a challenge. Some say they want to be rich, but they really don't know what that means. In a sense, to paraphrase the Italian Renaissance polymath Leonardo da Vinci, many are like ships on the high seas of life without rudders! They have tremendous potential but no direction. This troubles us.

One of the intrinsic rewards of being a professor is having the opportunity to be in contact with former students. Often they are willing to provide retrospective commentaries and share their trials and tribulations with their mentors. Some of our students have become hugely successful: positive family life, rich career, and enjoy good health. Some, as you might suspect, are disenfranchised. They are bitter about their education and the lack of preparation it provided, among other things. It seems that they are quick to blame others for their situation rather than themselves. No doubt there is plenty of blame to assign. Clearly we did not impart the right lessons forcibly enough to this group.

As parents, we want our children and grandchildren to be guided on the "right" path. We want the same for our former and current students, as we view them as our sons and daughters in a figurative sense. We hope to inspire and to point all people in what we believe is the right direction. This direction has been tempered by over forty years of academic and consulting research on what it really means to be rich. Our approach relies heavily on tried-and-true social science research methods of personal interviews and large-scale structured surveys. In other words, we have more than our personal opinions to offer.

In preparing this book—conducting personal interviews and collecting a nationwide sample of high net worth homeowners—it became clear that "the God factor" and spirituality could not be ignored. In fact, the role God plays in one's life is critical to being richer than a mere millionaire. This is particularly true in our society, which has been built upon a foundation of Judeo/Christian ethics and teachings.

While in graduate school, Bill Danko had the pleasure of studying under Professor Jim MacLachlan at Rensselaer Polytechnic Institute. Although Jim is no longer with us in this world, some of our meetings included seemingly out-of-place anecdotes and perspectives that resonate to this day. Not expecting it, Jim said he found God at Berkeley, where he earned his doctorate. And after he returned from a Harvard MBA reunion, he remarked: "Now I know why pride is a deadly sin." But it wasn't just these casual statements that were notable. In his all-too-short career, Jim published a very insightful article in the marketing literature about persuasion, focusing on twelve techniques based on well-studied psychological principles.[1] In this article, he cited a particular model of persuasive communication: the biblical parable of the good Samaritan (Luke 10:25–37). Noting that modern-day advertisements might contain several of the twelve persuasion techniques, he revealed that this parable contains all twelve. Jim concluded, "The mind of man is well understood by God who created him. It is not surprising, then, that when God communicates to man through his word he does so with technical excellence. The Bible is a source of communication ideas [that] has been used by great writers for centuries." For this reason, we too reference this important source to gain true understanding of what it means to be rich.[2]

OUR PURPOSE

As educators, parents, and grandparents, we have extensively searched—and researched—for answers to two questions: What does it mean to be richer than a millionaire? And how does one reach that status? Although we reveal our findings for a likely pathway to true prosperity, it is important to recognize that, regardless of wealth accumulation, all of us are merely custodians of the material things in our lives.

The purpose of this book is to help readers (especially young people about to embark on life's journey) answer this very question: Is being a millionaire even a worthy goal? If the answer is yes, this book offers guidelines and inspiration for the venture.

For most, it is a challenge to become a millionaire. But even if millionaire status is attained, there is no guarantee that satisfaction will follow. In fact—and as our empirical evidence shows—it is possible to hold a modest financial net worth and be very happy. All things considered, being rich and happy is not a bad goal; it is the American dream. In our view, being modestly wealthy (in a material sense) *and* happy is a very close second. It is difficult to imagine a life without happiness, no matter the level of financial net worth.

SURVEY RESEARCH

A total of 1,354 homeowners with a minimum net worth of $100,000 provided usable data through a four-page "paper and pencil" questionnaire. (Details of the sample composition are shown in the appendix.) Purposively, low financial net worth respondents were excluded, so as not to confound comparisons and interpretations. This is an important consideration, as a study found "that the negative impact of the goal for financial success on overall life satisfaction diminished as household income increased."[3] Thus, it is imperative to exclude those more likely to be struggling financially. Further, renters were also excluded, as the primary mailing list targeted homeowners, namely those with addresses more likely to be permanent. This should not pose a problem since the majority of America's affluent are homeowners.

The sample yields two main groups: up-and-comers (sometime referred to as the "mass affluent") with a household net worth under $1 million but over $100,000 (n=557) and millionaires with a net worth of $1 million or more (n=797). A first cut of the two major groups provides an interesting framework. Within each major group, two subsets can be formed based on responses to a measure of life satisfaction. This framework allows for four mutually exclusive and independent samples: dissatisfied up-and-comers (n=120), satisfied up-and-comers (n=408), dissatisfied millionaires (n=84), and satisfied millionaires (n=699). The usable sample size comprised from the four groups is n=1,311. Because of the need to omit those with "neutral satisfaction"—those who are neither satisfied nor dissatisfied—fourteen millionaires and twenty-nine up-and-comers could not be classified but will be included in some of the other analyses that follow. Select household financial characteristics for these four groups are shown in Table I-1.

Table I-1
Select Household Financial Characteristics
(in Thousands) for Four Survey Groups

Characteristic	Survey Group			
	1	2	3	4
	"up-and-comers"		millionaires	
	Dissatisfied	Satisfied	Dissatisfied	Satisfied
	n=120	n=408	n=84	n=699
Income				
Median	$90	$150	$150	$250
Average	$127	$162	$242	$353
Net Worth				
Median	$350	$800	$1,750	$1,750
Average	$571	$622	$2,473	$4,109
Home Value				
Median	$400	$473	$750	$800
Average	$480	$531	$804	$1,057
Debt				
Median	$160	$195	$200	$200
Average	$189	$234	$275	$306
Debt/Net Worth	33.10%	37.60%	11.10%	7.40%

Clearly there are financial differences among the groups. However, all four groups have average incomes that place them in the top 20 percent of all income producers in the United States. And all have substantial net worth. Satisfied up-and-comers (Group 2) have half of the median net worth and one-quarter the average net worth of the dissatisfied millionaires (Group 3) but three times the debt-to-net-worth ratio. This gives another clue that satisfaction and material wealth are not necessarily positively related to each other.

In sum, each of the survey respondents is quite well off financially. However, their lifestyles are markedly different in important ways, tempered by personal values, which will be explored later.

In addition to the survey research, we include vignettes of millionaires and up-and-comers, either who we interviewed or who were made known to us, and personal letters requesting advice.

Throughout this book our research findings are presented along with behavioral advice to those who want to become millionaires and reach the coveted goal of true prosperity, which we define as good health, happiness, and wealth.

HOW WE MEASURE SATISFACTION

Measuring satisfaction or subjective well-being (SWB)[4] is well established in the psychology literature. The measure we use is detailed in chapter 5. You can calculate your personal SWB score for comparison to others.

THE MILLION-DOLLAR QUESTION

And now, the million-dollar question: In which group will you end up? What follows will help you understand the qualities of each group. Here is a foreshadowing of what is to come: groups 1 and 3 (the dissatisfied) and groups 2 and 4 (the satisfied), as couplets, are more similar to each other than are 1 with 2 and 3 with 4, which are based on net worth. In other words, money alone doesn't make you rich.

The first four chapters of this book cover material wealth formation. The next three chapters focus on happiness, how to reach true prosperity, and whether building a dynasty is even possible. In the last chapter we reflect on lessons learned and where we go from here.

CHAPTER 1

WHO WANTS TO BE A MILLIONAIRE?

Is being a millionaire even a worthy goal? In all likelihood, most people would answer this question with a resounding YES. If this is your choice and you haven't yet reached that lofty goal, then read on to learn how others have attained financial success. However, the bigger inquiry and prime focus of this book is identifying what it takes to reach true prosperity and clearly become richer than a millionaire.

ARE YOU ALL IN?

If you really want to be a millionaire *and* reach true prosperity, it is likely that some behavior modification will be required as revealed in each chapter. Try to follow the advice provided in this book of well-adjusted millionaires and proceed along the pathway blazed by them to improve your chances of reaching your desired destination. Is it foolproof? No. Will it increase your chances? Yes.

Millionaires are defined by net worth—that is, the difference between assets and liabilities. About three of every twenty-five households in America are millionaire households. However, it is important to note that asset classes vary. Commercial real estate, for example, may generate income and appreciate in value over time, while allowing tax-deductible property and school taxes and maintenance costs. On the other hand, liquid equities may pay a reliable quarterly dividend. The wealthy typically hold both kinds of assets: those that create cash flow and those with a long-term payoff.

Consider the wisdom of 1985 Nobel Laureate Franco Modigliani, who won the prize in economics for his life cycle of money theory. In effect, he concluded that, when you are young, you work for money, and when you are old, money works for you by paying interest and dividends. Of note, Benjamin Franklin understood this. He was able to retire from commerce at the age of forty-two, devoting the latter part of his life to science and public service, all while living off of his earlier investments.

If you are now or ever plan to be a millionaire, it is prudent for retirement planning to consume 4 percent or less of invested assets after you retire. This "burn rate" will practically ensure that you will not outlive your assets. Thus 4 percent of a million dollars yields $40,000 annually, which is an income below the national median. Of course, the rates of return on investments and resulting tax liabilities must be part of the disbursement equation. In any event, this should give you a wake-up call about what it means to be a millionaire on the low end of the spectrum (although no one should feel sorry for the millionaire who can't generate enough retirement income). A million-dollar net worth is just the starting point on your journey to financial independence. Besides retirement, money provides options for quality housing, safe neighborhoods, cars, college tuition, charity, and vacations, along with so many other things in the world. Studies have also revealed that wealth can enhance happiness.

In their study of the relationship between happiness and income, two researchers found that of those who earn between $20,000 and $30,000, 52 percent are *fairly happy*, and of those who earn between $75,000 and $100,000, 60 percent are *very happy*. Further, it was learned that of those who earned more than $500,000, 100 percent are *very happy!*[5] So, yes, having many financial resources will help with overall peace of mind. After all, not being stressed over meeting financial obligations is a fortunate position. Financial security rather than just money itself affords a feeling of well-being. A paycheck that does more than cover living expenses provides a sense of individuality, and it provides a means to save and to invest. A well-suited career that produces sufficient income sets the stage for happiness.

Of course, some will spend everything they earn and more. Such practices are examples of having money available for now but ignoring the building of a sustainable, financially secure future. This characterizes the under accumulators as highlighted in *The Millionaire Next Door.*[6]

Many mistakenly believe that most wealthy people inherited their wealth. It is important to understand that the vast majority of millionaires in America actually earned their wealth.

Certainly compound interest and/or good returns on investments are important for creating wealth. It is also important to have a good income to invest over time. How do those who will one day become economically self-sufficient do it?

Many of the lessons have been known for at least 250 years.[7] Benjamin Franklin told us that taxes and governmental regulation are but ten percent of our burden. The major reason some are wealthy is due to *personal initiative.* In other words, Franklin believed in meritocracy. What are you as an individual going to do with your talents to add value in exchange for money?

ADVICE FROM "WELL-ADJUSTED" MILLIONAIRES

Through our research, informed by Benjamin Franklin and others, we have identified the key factors that are required for wealth formation. Please note, however, this is not a formula for guaranteed success.

Instead look at this advice as a set of building blocks that make it more likely that you will become wealthy. Further, we emphasize the words "well adjusted," since it is possible to be rich and miserable—a condition to be avoided. Embracing some while ignoring others of the traits is at your peril.

1. CREATE A GOOD WORK ETHIC BY BEING INDUSTRIOUS—HAVE A PASSION

Having a good work ethic and a motivating passion results in a powerful commitment to mission. It is essential to have goals and objectives. Goals are set based on what we want to achieve. Objectives are the precise and measurable steps taken in order to reach our goals.

Vignette: Bobby K.

Bobby K. is twenty-one years old. He was an outstanding student throughout his high school years. He found his passion in mechanical technology as a young boy. His favorite gifts were remote controlled cars, which he would dissect and modify to enable quicker and more accurate performance. In high school, he joined a robotics team and participated with others in building robots for competitions. His skills were a perfect match for effectively driving the robot during competitive meetings, and his team had many successes in regional and national competitions.

Although he was awarded partial scholarships to major private engineering universities, he chose a community college with an articulation agreement with his first university choice. The agreement allowed transfer entry with full junior status after the two-year degree completion if he maintained a grade point average of at least 3.8 (out of 4.0). He chose this pathway because of tuition cost savings. His hope—then and now—is to not accumulate massive student loans. He met the criteria, and again, he was awarded scholarship funding for his second two years. Because of his passion to work in the field of robotics, he chose as his program of study mechanical and aeronautical engineering.

Bobby's *objectives* are clear: complete his engineering degrees, continue with paying internships, attend graduate school (the company with which he would work would pay part of his graduate studies), and after completion of his graduate degree, enter the job market. His *goal* is to design and build robots.

Bobby has demonstrated a solid work ethic and commitment to his goal. Further, he has been conservative in terms of financing his education. He is self-reliant and will not be burdened with mountains of debt after graduation. He has persevered and plans to continue on that profitable pathway.

Having taught thousands of students, if we were gamblers, we would bet that Bobby K. will be a self-actualized success.

2. Persevere—There Is No Gain without Pain

In Table 1-1, we list some members on the Forbes 400 List of wealthy individuals. While some might be familiar names from the news, and others more obscure, each individual on the list can be described as being industrious and persevering in a wide variety of undertakings.

The commonality among the members of this list is their individual initiative, even at the corporate level. In a study that sought to find whether groups or individuals mattered more in developing radical innovations (namely, the next new profitable blockbuster), the authors concluded: "The firms participating in our study earnestly wanted radical innovation to follow a systematic, organization-driven process. However, we found just the opposite: *radical innovation was primarily driven by individual initiative.* We were surprised by the lack of corporate attention…"[8]

Table 1-1
Select Members on the Forbes 400 List

Sheldon Adelson	Casinos
Micky Arison	Carnival Cruises
Steve Ballmer	Microsoft
Jeff Bezos	Amazon.com
Brian Chesky	Airbnb
Jim Davis	New Balance
Larry Ellison	Oracle
Diane Hendricks	ABC Supply
Herbert Kohler, Jr.	Plumbing fixtures
Phil Knight	Nike
George Lucas	Star Wars
Bernard Marcus	Home Depot
Elon Musk	Tesla Motors
Pierre Omidyar	eBay
Larry Page	Google
Steven Spielberg	Movies
Ronda Stryker	Stryker, Inc.
Jim Walton	Wal-Mart
Mark Zuckerberg	Facebook

ACT LIKE AN OLYMPIAN

Most people will never be Olympians. However, we can practice one of their traits: never quit trying. Olympians are tenacious participants, as demonstrated by the following exchange from Nancy Hogshead, the most decorated swimmer in the 1984 Olympic Games:[9]

> A 90-year-old man came up to me after one of my talks and said, "I could have been in the Olympics. It's just that I got in a fight with my coach."
>
> I was raised to respect my elders, but I wanted to tell him, "If you let a fight with your coach get between you and the Olympics—you weren't even close. You've been kidding yourself for the past seventy years."

BRIEF PROFILES OF PERSEVERING WEALTH BUILDERS

- James Dyson, born in 1947, studied at the Royal College of Art from 1966 through 1970, then pursued engineering. He learned determination as a long distance runner, allowing him to build 5,127 prototypes of the Dyson G-Force vacuum cleaner before it was introduced to the market in 1983. Forbes estimates his net worth at over $4 billion.[10]

- Raymond Dolby (1933–2013) earned a PhD in physics from Cambridge and founded Dolby Labs in the UK in 1965. He moved to San Francisco in 1967. The 1971 movie *A Clockwork Orange* was the first to use Dolby sound filtering. At the time of his death, his net worth was $2.85 billion. The publicly traded DLB stock has a market value of $5.33 billion.[11]

- Angie Hicks was born in 1970 and holds a Harvard MBA. She cofounded "Angie's List" in 1995 when she "needed decent contractors." When asked what she has learned about herself while running her business, she replied: "One of my strongest traits is perseverance. It has helped me accomplish things I never dreamt of being able to do, like selling door to door."[12] The publicly traded ANGI stock has a market value of $739 million.

- Ruth Fertel (1927–2002) attended Louisiana State University. In 1965 she bought her first "Ruth's Chris Steakhouse" by mortgaging her house. Her motive was to earn money to send her sons to college.[13] RUTH stock has a market value of $620 million.

There are many millionaires who are "intrapreneurs"—employees who are granted autonomy within their jobs such that they can act as entrepreneurs. This is beneficial for the company as well as for the individuals with an entrepreneurial spirit. But with the right commitment to achieving financial independence, you don't even need to be an entrepreneur or intrapreneur; just holding a well-paying, suitable job will enable wealth building.

3. Practice Good Stewardship

How efficient is it to make a lot of money only to have it taxed away? The best way to avoid this is by knowing the rules of the game. Based on press reports, Warren Buffett and Teresa Heinz Kerry know the rules. In 2006, Mr. Buffett, for example, was taxed at 17.7 percent on the $46 million he made.[14] Recall that when Mrs. Kerry released her 2003 tax return during her husband's bid for the presidency, it was revealed that she had $5.1 million of income; $2.8 million was from tax-free investments. Her total tax obligation was $750,000, or 14.7 percent on the total.[15]

These examples speak to the importance of good stewardship and having competent financial advisors. Consider that you may face up to a 39.6 percent federal income tax rate on earned income. And, if you are not careful, you may also get hit with a draconian death tax. Prudent individuals understand the value of donating their wealth to charity, even if it is to their own family foundation. This truth was expressed eloquently by a court of appeals judge in 1934: "Any one may so arrange his affairs that his taxes shall be as low as possible; he is not bound to choose that pattern which will best pay the Treasury; there is not even a patriotic duty to increase one's taxes."[16]

Most of those who have become wealthy and want to maintain their status will engage in a variety of asset-preservation strategies. They often have multiple streams of income: rents, interest, dividends, royalties, capital growth, and perhaps even earned income. Importantly, they minimize taxes by preferring capital gains and stock dividends over earned income; they seek long-term capital appreciation with real estate and often enjoy tax-free municipal bonds.

Minimizing taxes is an important part of good stewardship, but so is overseeing your own affairs in a general sense. The late Leonard Cohen, a Canadian singer-songwriter, was an extremely creative artist. Unfortunately, he had to sue those he trusted to manage his financial affairs because of their "greed, self-dealing, concealment, knowing misrepresentation and reckless disregard for professional fiduciary duties," according to a complaint filed in the Los Angeles Superior Court.[17] Fortunately, Mr. Cohen prevailed in court, winning $9 million, but he still could not retire at the age of 71 due to the enormous legal fees he incurred.[18] Despite this betrayal, he prayed for his ex-manager "that a spirit of understanding will convert her heart from hatred to remorse."[19]

4. Be Frugal

Benjamin Franklin noted that "it is easier to suppress the first desire than to satisfy all that follow it." One hundred years after Franklin, the fictional Mr. Micawber reinforced this idea in *David Copperfield*:

"Annual income twenty pounds, annual expenditure nineteen nineteen six, result happiness. Annual income twenty pounds, annual expenditure twenty pounds ought and six, result misery."[20] Think about it: you buy a new suit, so you "need" new shoes. The trick is to live below your means and invest across a diversified set of assets, such as stocks, bonds, and real estate.

Frugality requires us to live *below* our means (and not just *at* our means). If you make $70,000, live on $60,000. If you make $100,000, live on $80,000. We interviewed a physician making $400,000 annually, but because he is such a good credit risk at his bank, he lives on $450,000 annually. Do you think that this otherwise smart individual is frugal? Could you live on $320,000 annually while saving twenty percent of a $400,000 income? Can he retire without drastically adjusting his lifestyle?

Vignette: Disciplined Financial Adaption

After six years in his job as a civil engineer, John W., thirty-one years old, becomes a victim of downsizing. He and his wife, Ellen, are homeowners with a mortgage. Given the job environment, opportunities look bleak for him. His wife is an employed physician's assistant with solid job security. Now on just one income and after many discussions, they decide to go forward with tightly controlled spending using an austerity budget. In their opinion, this is essential for financial survival.

After carefully reviewing all prior expenditures, they mutually decide what to reduce or completely eliminate. Of course, some choices are more difficult than others. They dub their new prudently crafted budget the "austerity plan."

Ellen's income coupled with unemployment insurance for John is sufficient for sustainability of their new lifestyle until John is able to secure a job. Their plan shows income and expenses as balanced. The adopted plan follows the guidelines of the "Do's and Don'ts of Financial Belt Tightening,"[21] summarized in Table 1-2.

After seven months John is able to find a job in the same city with a slight increase in pay from his previous position. Now, his income is fully restored to the level prior to his layoff. John and Ellen revisit their budget with the amended income and conclude that their interim budget has been suitable for their reformed comfort zone. Consequently, they decide to save or invest 60 percent of John's salary for wealth building, with a comfortable retirement as a goal. Although the misfortune of a job loss arose, pragmatic planning and rethinking of frivolous spending led to awareness that less can be more in the long run. Construction of a pathway to prosperity engenders a conduit to happiness.

Reality check: none of us can work forever. It pays to be frugal.

Table 1-2
The Do's and Don'ts of Financial Belt Tightening

Do

Prepare and use budgets
Avoid credit card usage
Avoid discretionary spending
Give new meaning to the word frugal
Seek alternative employment
Maintain your pragmatic sense of humor

Don't

Ignore the seriousness of the situation
Wait too long to prepare an action plan
Pretend everything is the same
Forget to take time out

5. Avoid Excessive Debt

According to the IRS, the average millionaire at time of death had a debt/equity ratio of 7.4 percent. In a recent nationwide survey of living millionaires, we found the debt/equity ratio ranged from 0 to 12 percent. It seems that most millionaires avoid excessive debt.

Benjamin Franklin wrote 250 years ago in "The Way to Wealth" that "the borrower is a slave to the lender." This same warning can be found in the biblical book of Proverbs (22:7), which was written 2,500 years ago. This is timeless wisdom.

This one issue—excessive debt—has devastated many families and is largely caused by easy credit. Not only is credit easy to obtain, but we are also strongly encouraged to use it. Credit charges are readily made for consumable products such as groceries, beverages, and even fast food. Food products that have been consumed are paid for at a later date, with interest charges accumulating for thirty days or more into the future. Avoidance of placing readily consumable or frivolous purchases on credit cards is the best practice.

Interest rates on credit cards are extreme, especially as compared with interest rates on savings and certificates of deposit. "Average rates… [are] closer to 14 percent as of the fourth quarter of 2015. It is important to note that while average rates paid by consumers have moved in a relatively narrow band over the past several years, interest rates charged vary considerably across credit card plans and borrowers, reflecting the various features of the plans and the risk profile of the card holders served."[22]

Credit card debt is an enabler to live beyond one's means and to provide a channel to immediate gratification of a perceived need or want. The problem of instant gratification, with a charge today and pay tomorrow mentality, is that it will lead to a stack of debts accompanied by exorbitant interest and other charges. Be prudent, and live below (not just within) your means by being frugal and avoiding excessive debt. Refer to chapter 6 and the discussion on spending reduction issues coupled with viable actions for avoiding excessive debt.

6. Be Humble

In "The Way to Wealth," Benjamin Franklin wrote: "Do not depend too much upon your own industry, and frugality, and prudence, though excellent things; for they may all be blasted, without the blessing of Heaven; and, therefore, ask that blessing humbly." Being humble requires us to recognize that our success is a gift.

7. Be Charitable

Franklin advises us to share our wealth with the less fortunate. This is sound advice. Indeed, all major religions require charity:

- Judaism: Sharing your bread with the hungry, sheltering the oppressed and the homeless; Clothing the naked when you see them, and not turning your back on your own. (Isaiah 58:7)

- Christianity: Lord, when did we see you hungry or thirsty or a stranger or naked or ill or in prison, and not minister to your needs? He will answer them, Amen I say to you, what you did not do for one of these least ones, you did not do for me. (Matthew 25:44–45)

- Islam: One of the 5 pillars of Islam is giving alms to the needy.

- Hinduism: [The highest form of] Charity that is given as a matter of duty, to a deserving candidate who does nothing in return, at the right place and time, is called a Saattvika charity. (Bhagavad Gita, Chapter XVII)

Our data show that givers of time and money, regardless of religion, and those who practice the Golden Rule, are happier. This is further explored in chapter 5.

8. Have a Good Marriage

It all begins with a couple's selection in the partnering process and, hopefully, constructively builds from there. Most marriage counselors agree that open and honest communication is a necessary ingredient for a successful marriage. Wedding vows are a formal spoken, and sometimes written, agreement between two parties. Although the vows may vary, the spoken words often include the idea immortalized in the phrase "to have and to hold, from this day forward, for better, for worse, for richer, for poorer, in sickness and in health, until death do us part." These are very powerful words if placed into practice.

Of course, a successful marriage is not always realized with the first attempt or even others that follow. Such situations are explored later in this book. Further, although a successful marriage makes wealth building more probable, being single certainly does not preclude achieving prosperity. It is noteworthy that a study by the Centers for Disease Control and Prevention suggests that married adults are healthier than divorced, widowed or never married adults.[23] The study finds that married adults are less likely than others to be in poor health and less likely to be limited in various activities, including work and other activities of daily living. Such status contributes to overall well-being. As a good example, the prolific writer Stephen King gives the secret of his success as having a stable marriage and staying physically healthy. [24]

9. HAVE GOOD HEALTH

As Bobby McFerrin sang in 1998, "Don't Worry, Be Happy" is a philosophy of sorts. Research indicates that a sense of feeling good about oneself generates favorable outcomes. Staying positive and remaining hopeful even during stressful periods leads to greater happiness. Guarded optimism is better than pessimism.

Physical fitness is a worthy goal. Feeling good about yourself, a desire that can be enhanced through moderate exercise, will contribute to improved self-esteem.[25] Physical fitness is of lasting benefit when it becomes an integral part of your lifestyle. A healthy lifestyle enables you to work longer and generate more income to save and invest.

10. HAVE A GOOD INCOME

Education is derived from many sources—not only from college degrees, but also from technical training programs, apprentice training, and certifications. Whatever your chosen field, you must always be receptive to lifelong learning. Moreover, as shown in *The Millionaire Next Door*, significant wealth accumulation is entirely possible with nearly any reasonable income. You do not have to be a physician or an attorney to know that longevity and consistent behavior that embraces frugality and avoids debt will enable you to move forward on the pathway to prosperity. You must become a saver and an investor. Table 1-3 provides a summary of job growth and salaries along with forecasts for future opportunities.

Table 1-3
Fastest Growing Occupations, 2014-2024
(Numbers in Thousands)

Occupation	2014	2024	2014 Wage	Entry Education
Wind turbine service techs	4.4	9.2	$48,800	Some college
Occupational therapy assistant	33.0	47.1	$56,950	Associate's
Physical therapist assistant	78.7	110.7	$54,410	Associate's
Physical therapist aides	50.0	69.5	$24,650	High school
Home health aides	913.5	1,261.9	$21,380	Informal
Commercial divers	4.4	6.0	$45,890	Special
Nurse practitioners	126.9	171.7	$95,350	Master's
Physical therapists	210.9	282.7	$82,390	Doctoral
Statisticians	30.0	40.1	$79,990	Master's
Ambulance drivers	19.6	26.1	$24,080	High school
Occupational therapy aides	8.8	11.6	$26,550	High school
Physician assistants	94.4	123.2	$95,820	Master's
Operations research analysts	91.3	118.9	$76,660	Bachelor's
Personal financial advisors	249.4	323.2	$81,060	Bachelor's
Cartographers	12.3	15.9	$60,930	Bachelor's

Source: US Bureau of Labor Statistics

Getting Personal

Dear Drs. WDD and RVN,

I've been a full- and part-time student without a college degree for the past ten years. I know that not having a degree is holding me back from job advancement. So far, I have accumulated 186 credit hours with an overall GPA of 3.2. Since my job requires travel and relocations, I keep changing majors as often as I change schools.

I'd like to finish all this undergraduate college stuff and move on to a graduate degree program, perhaps an MBA. Do you have any suggestions to expedite degree completion?

Sincerely,
Learned Lenny

Dear Lenny,

Sure! You have demonstrated that you can successfully handle course work—and lots of it. You need to enroll in an online degree program. The first step is to review your college transcripts and determine where the most credits were earned. Since you have met residency requirements (or at least in part), you should look to those institutions first.

Check the institution's online degree offerings. Most colleges and universities offer online courses, and there is a trend to offer complete online degree programs. Of course, if a program is fully online, then no physical residency is required.

Given your job demands of travel and relocation, an online option is ideal for you. After you complete undergraduate degree requirements (which may be relatively easy given your earned credit hours), you may want to consider an online MBA.

To further reinforce the significance of education, Table 1-4 shows median (as many above as below) weekly earnings and unemployment rates based on educational attainment. Clearly, education pays if selection is based on career choice with a focus on economic well-being. Of course, the highest-paying career is not always within one's desire or qualifications. In large part, we identify who we are with what work we do. So having a job that is congruent with your self-image will more likely lead to happiness.

Table 1-4
Earnings and Unemployment Rates
by Educational Attainment, 2015

Education	Median Usual Weekly Earnings	Unemployment Rate
Doctoral degree	$ 1,623	1.70%
Professional degree	$ 1,730	1.50%
Master's degree	$ 1,341	2.40%
Bachelor's degree	$ 1,137	2.80%
Associate's degree	$ 798	3.80%
Some college, no degree	$ 738	5.00%
High school diploma	$ 678	5.40%
Less than a high school diploma	$ 493	8.00%
All workers	$ 860	4.30%

Note: Data are for persons age twenty-five and over.
Earnings are for full-time and salary workers.

Source: US Bureau of Labor Statistics

Some people reason that if they only got into the right school, they would be better off financially. This is not always true. Consider two examples. *The Wall Street Journal* reported about a somber Harvard Law School reunion. "Many members of the class of '85 are still reeling. They feel trapped, and don't see where their careers are going to go. Many of them had never experienced failure and had presumed their elite degree would be a lifetime annuity."[26] In a broader sense, two researchers concluded that student ambition is a better predictor of earning success than what college they ultimately choose.[27]

Getting Personal

Dear Drs. WDD and RVN,

I am twenty years old, and right after high school graduation, I moved from Upstate New York to California in search of my dream job of working on the creation of graphic novels. Well, things aren't working out so well. It's expensive here, and available jobs are in the service sector at very low entry-level pay or in sales with pay based entirely on commission. It appears that a degree is necessary to break into the job that I really am interested in. I am not a quitter, but I am stressed out with this reality check. I'd like to do what I set out to do, and I want to be a success financially. It doesn't look like I'm on the right pathway. Maybe I need a reset? Any advice?

Sincerely,
Frustrated Graphic Novelist

Dear Novelist,

A regrouping and then a reset would be a good move. Education is essential for most of the technically sophisticated jobs in your chosen industry. There are entire college programs that prepare students to enter your desired career field. Look into online educational opportunities that serve your needs. Perhaps a cost-efficient community college near your hometown is the best starting point. In regard to living costs, have you considered returning home where your costs would be reduced, especially related to education in a public institution, given residency requirements?

You are twenty years old and not a quitter, so YES, follow your dream—but streamline the costs. We see the attractiveness of your chosen career. Control your overall costs and go for it!

This lesson has broad implications for all of us. Participate and—no matter what transpires—don't give up. Read on.

Getting Personal

Dear Drs. WDD and RVN,

We are a family of four. All is going well, in spite of several financial setbacks caused by a three-month period of unemployment. My husband and I, in all ways, hold the family value of supportiveness very high.

Our kids are doing very well in school. Thankfully, we are all healthy and pleased with our current overall situation. Our financial net worth is about $750,000.

Our question is in regard to the current economy. Neither my husband nor I have truly secure jobs. Is there any time-tested approach to prepare for job loss along with the financial and emotional impact that would follow?

Thank you,
Concerned Wife and Mother

Dear Concerned,

It is great to hear all is going so well with you and your family. Indeed it is important to recognize that nothing has 100 percent certainty except, as we are too often reminded, death and taxes. However, other than those two dismal facts, most other aspects of life are open to alternative choices.

Lifelong employment within one organization is an elusive concept. Most people will have three career changes that will include multiple job changes. It is extremely important to keep your job skills updated and to sincerely subscribe to the commitment of lifelong learning.

If and when job loss occurs, having an austerity budget drafted and keeping your resume current, your confidence level will be elevated. Just be sure to remember: BE PRAGMATIC.

THE LABOR FORCE

While it might seem obvious, to build wealth you need to earn income. However, it's not always obvious to everyone. Case in point: LFPR.

The Bureau of Labor Statistics[28] tracks the civilian labor force participation rate (LFPR). This participation rate is an important measure because the unemployment rate that is published each month only includes those who are seeking work. A low unemployment rate suggests that the economy is healthy; more people are employed. However, this is only part of the story. What about the portion of people who have given up, who are not looking for work?

In January 1948, the LFPR was 58.6 percent. In 2000 it was 67.3 percent, and in 2008, 66.2 percent. In January 2016, just 62.7 percent of the 158,335,000 members of the unemployed labor force of at least sixteen years of age were seeking work. This means 99,276,045 people were seeking work, and 59,058,955 people had given up. How can that be healthy for them as individuals or for our country?

The bottom line: you need a reliable source of income to build wealth. In chapter 2, we examine perceptions and measurement of wealth.

HOW MUCH IS ENOUGH?

WHAT IS RICH?

A wise man once remarked: "I have all the money I need if I die today." True enough, but suppose you don't die today. Would you feel you had enough wealth to meet your future needs? An MSN Money poll suggests that to feel rich one needs a $5 million net worth.[29] Northern Trust, using Federal Reserve data, asserts that "Beer & Pretzels" rich (which is a nickname for entry-level superrich) requires a net worth of $25 million to $50 million, a hurdle that can be met by less than 125,000 households.[30]

Our study[31] provides insight about how much one needs to *feel* rich. In brief, as shown in Figure 2-1, to feel rich one always needs more than one currently has. Responses to two survey questions were used to construct the graph. Self-reported current net worth ranged from $100,000 to over $20,000,000. The follow-up question asked how much would be needed to feel rich. The data show that whatever you have, the more you think you need to feel rich, as shown by the bigger multiplier. Fortunately, the more you have, you only think you need slightly more, as shown by the relatively smaller multiplier. So, if your current net worth is $500,000, to feel rich, you "need" five times as much, or $2,500,000. If your net worth is $5,000,000, to feel rich, you "need" 1.6 times as much, or $8,000,000.[32]

It would be interesting to assess the sentiments of the 1,800 worldwide billionaires. Would their multiplier be less than one? More importantly, this exercise demonstrates that perception matters. Feeling rich is a state of mind.

Figure 2-1
How Much Does One "Need" To Feel Rich?

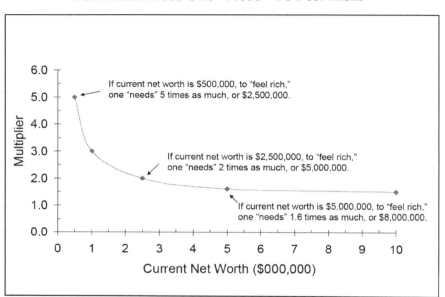

It is important to understand that everything that follows depends on living in an environment that allows for wealth formation. We examine net worth, as revealed on a balance sheet, in the next section.

HOW TO SPEAK CONVERSATIONAL ACCOUNTING

Accounting is the language of finance and is used, in most cases, as a basis for decision making. "Accounting speak" is a way of expressing the effects of transactions. Succinctly, accounting tracks income (what is earned), assets (what is owned), liabilities (what is owed), and net worth (assets minus liabilities).

It is important to understand some of the language because it affects much of our lives in terms of wealth building and tax obligations. For those in the business world, the language is much more extensive and can involve complex recording of transactions.

For now, let's consider an individual's balance sheet.

WHAT BELONGS ON THE BALANCE SHEET?

The financial report card is the balance sheet. Typically, assets are listed in order of liquidity—that is, how easily an asset can be accessed as cash. An example of this order is as follows: cash, checking account balances, savings, and receivables. Next are the liabilities, short- and long-term, which include such things as credit card balances, car loans, and mortgages. The difference between total assets and total liabilities is net worth.

Now, consider the value of revenue generators such as social security. In recent years discussions have begun as to whether sources of payments such as social security are assets. There are strong arguments for both positions. Technically, one's social security account cannot be sold as could stocks or bonds. However, social security payments, which are in fact an annuity, do provide constant income with an adjustment for inflation. Social security is not a financial resource that may be liquidated. Payments are spread over a person's lifetime after meeting certain qualifications. Although the payments end with the death of the recipient, if there is a surviving spouse, then there may be entitlement to acquire the deceased's payment in lieu of the survivor's own if it is of greater value.

One approach to placing an approximate value on social security income is to divide a reasonable current rate of return into the annual payments. For example, how much would have to be invested to generate one's current annual social security income? Assuming payments totaling $30,000 for the year and using a rate of return of 4 percent, the assigned value would be the sum of $30,000/.04, which is $750,000.

Others may choose to calculate the net present value of the distributions. Of course, there are discussions of the longevity of the social security system itself, whether or not there will be "needs testing" in the future, increased age restriction for full benefits, and possible payment reductions.

We have invested money into the system along with our employer's matching contributions. We rightfully expect a return. Again, some may argue that social security is at best a perceived asset, but no one can argue that these funds aren't redistributed into the economy through purchased goods, services, and perhaps savings, but whatever the distribution, an economic impact results. In 2015, over 59 million Americans received almost $870 billion in social security benefits.[33]

Even in the midst of arguments over whether social security or other similar income generators should be included on a balance sheet, the fact remains that such resources provide income. Social security income is a necessary and large component of household income for older retirees as indicated in the data that follow.

- Among households with consumers age fifty-five and over in 2014, wages and salaries represented 76 percent of income before taxes for those ages fifty-five to sixty-four; 42.9 percent for those ages sixty-five to seventy-four; and 14.9 percent for those age seventy-five and older. For those age seventy-five years and older, social security and private and government retirement represented 70.5 percent of income before taxes. This compared with 46.1 percent for those ages sixty-five to seventy-four and 10.3 percent for those ages fifty-five to sixty-four.

- Among all age groups in 2014, households with consumers ages fifty-five to sixty-four had the highest share of income before taxes in self-employment income (8.3 percent). Those under the age of twenty-five and those age seventy-five and older had the lowest (2 percent).[34]

All things considered, if a balance sheet is structured to include such revenue generators as assets, then these resources should be source qualified and considered for personal planning purposes only. Such inclusion should not be done while doing the suggested net worth comparative analysis that follows.

WHAT TO DO NEXT

The first step to measure your current wealth-building standing is to prepare a balance sheet. List all of your assets, together with their values, and total the listing. List all of your short-term and long-term liabilities, and total this listing. The difference between the two is your net worth.

Now you may compare your net worth with others.

According to the Federal Reserve, for all families in 2013, the median net worth was $81,200 and the mean (average) net worth was $534,600. The impact of age and education levels of the head of household on median and mean net worth are shown in Tables 2-1 and 2-2.

Table 2-1
Net Worth (in Thousands of Dollars)
by Age

Age of Head of Household	Net Worth	
	Median	Mean
Less than 35	10.4	75.5
35-44	46.7	347.0
45-54	105.3	530.1
55-64	165.9	798.4
65-74	232.1	1,057.0
75+	194.8	645.2

Source: Federal Reserve Bulletin, September 2014

Table 2-2
Net Worth (in Thousands of Dollars)
by Education Level

Education of Head of Household	Net Worth	
	Median	Mean
No high school diploma	17.2	108.3
High school diploma	52.5	199.6
Some college	46.9	317.9
College degree	219.4	1,031.6

Source: Federal Reserve Bulletin, September 2014

Clearly, education and age matter. Formal education provides a key advantage for professional employment possibilities. The good fortune of longevity provides an investor or saver with more time for wealth accumulation through compounding.

Whatever your financial position, there is always a chance for improvement in America.

AMERICA IS THE LAND OF OPPORTUNITY

Where is the wealth of nations? The World Bank answered that question in 2005 by examining the economic well-being of 120 countries. They found that 5 percent of a country's wealth can be attributed to natural resources, another 18 percent from production, but the majority of the wealth—77 percent—comes from "intangible capital residual." This last factor is a function of cultural values: investment in "rule of law" and "human capital" through education. Combined, the intangible capital residual consists of the skills and know-how of the labor force, trust among people, ability to work together for a common purpose, an efficient judicial system, clear property rights, and an effective government. Overall, rule of law explains nearly 60 percent of the intangible factor, and human capital accounts for approximately 35 percent.[35]

This finding is supported by a 2008 study of sixty-one countries to learn which were the most attractive to migrants. It found that countries that had a high standard of living, well-entrenched rule of law, educational opportunities, and a society that promoted free enterprise and competition were most attractive to those seeking a better life. The top five countries found most attractive (starting with the most) were the United States, the United Kingdom, Australia, Norway, and France. The least attractive of the sixty-one (starting with the least) were Venezuela, Nigeria, Cote D'Ivoire, Ghana, and Iran.[36]

Vignette: American Opportunity

We interviewed Enrique, a Mexican immigrant. He provides a good example of how to achieve the dream of financial freedom through hard work. Enrique has no formal education, but he does have perfect musical pitch. He is a piano tuner and a commissioned salesman for a piano company. He is able to expertly tune clients' pianos and then, in the privacy of their homes, engage them in a conversation about their piano needs. Enrique never took a marketing course, but he understands that focusing on the needs of his customers is a sure way to wealth. He has taken his stream of commissions from the sales and invested in real estate. Currently his net worth is $3 million. His last words in our interview: "America is the land of opportunity. If an uneducated immigrant can make it here, anyone can. God bless America!"

We are fortunate to live in America: the land of opportunity. However, not everyone takes advantage of the opportunities presented. Consequently, household wealth varies considerably. Of note, our study shows that the vast majority of millionaires (96 percent) agree with the following statement: America is the land of financial opportunity.

Further, most millionaires earned their wealth in one generation; they did not rely on an inheritance. Based on our survey of 797 millionaires, fully two-thirds inherited nothing. Nearly 90 percent of millionaires inherited less than 20 percent of their net worth. Conversely, 10 percent of millionaires inherited more than 20 percent of their net worth.

Let's look at some hands-on considerations for wealth accumulation.

THE POWER OF COMPOUNDING

While there are many paths to riches, anyone can grow a fortune given enough time. The Rule of 72 shows how long it takes to double your money. For example, if you can earn a 10 percent return after taxes and expenses, your money will double in approximately 7.2 years (72/10=7.2). While 10 percent may be quite optimistic, it illustrates the concepts of time and rates of return. Consider these examples:

- In 1626, the Dutch purchased Manhattan for twenty-four dollars. In 2005, 379 years later, the assessed value of all the properties in Manhattan was reported to be $186 billion. What was the annualized return? 6.19 percent.[37] This shows that even modest returns and a long time horizon can produce massive wealth.

- Suppose you received $10,000 at birth. What are the likely outcomes if the funds are placed into a savings account yielding 1.5 percent or invested in a broad stock market index fund that has historically yielded 8 percent annually? Saving it would result in a total value of $26,320 at age sixty-five. Not a very encouraging outcome. However, the same $10,000 for the same period of time, invested with an average annual rate of return of 8 percent, would yield $1,488,000. Major difference!

If you were not so lucky as to be given a gift of $10,000 at birth, is there hope of becoming a millionaire? Yes! The illustration in Table 2-3 shows how much one would have to save each month beginning at age twenty-five to amass over $1 million by age sixty-five, assuming an annual average 8 percent return compounded monthly. To contrast, notice how each ten-year age increment affects the outcome of accrued values.

Table 2-3
The Power of Compounding

Current Age	Monthly Savings	Total Value at Age 65
25	$325	$1,142,141
35	$325	$487,596
45	$325	$192,708
55	$325	$59,854
55	$5,800	$1,068,161

The lesson is clear: start saving at a young age, and let time work for you. It is probably far easier to save $325 each month when you are twenty-five than to save $5,800 each month when you are fifty-five to reach or go beyond the million-dollar goal. Of course, taxes must be considered and will reduce overall net accrual. Further, consideration must be given to the benefit of wealth building through tax-sheltered and tax-deferred investments. Also, risk tolerance must be taken into account in addition to inflationary effects. However, before anything else, a commitment to build a critical mass of funds is necessary for wealth creation.

While we trust you see the merits of consistently saving and investing money, it takes strong personal discipline to do it.

Getting Personal

Dear Drs. WDD and RVN,

I am a twenty-nine-year-old single woman and work as a paralegal in an elder care practice. Over the past four years, I have seen many good and too many unfortunate financial situations with our clients. To be sure, I don't want to wind up on the unfortunate side when I retire.

The law firm I work for has a generous salary and benefit package, and I truly like my job. Although I work with the legal side of asset protection, I am not so familiar with asset accumulation.

At present, I am able to invest $450 a month in my 401K plan, which is matched by my employer. Also, I receive a bonus, on average, of $3,000 each year, of which I put $2,500 into an IRA account. At this rate, am I on track to reach the status of millionaire when I retire?

Wondering Woman

Dear Wondering Woman,

It's great you like your job! Work you like along with a generous pay and benefit package is not so easy to find.

You don't mention your expenses. Are you accruing debt? Does your employer pay for your health care plan? Who will pay for this upon retirement? This will most likely be a major issue for retirement years.

As far as the retirement plan accounts are concerned, if you contribute $450 each month along with the same amount matched by the firm, then you are off to a good start. Assuming this aggressive investment plan holds, over the course of thirty-eight years (to reach the retirement age of sixty-seven) at a rate of return of 4 percent (compounded monthly), you will accrue $964,589 beyond what you may already have. This combined with your annual IRA contribution of $2,500, over thirty-eight years, with a 4 percent (compounded annually) return will add an additional $223,523.

So, yes, you are on track for a pool of funds exceeding $1,000,000. But remember that if you are happy and healthy and have sufficient means to maintain your chosen lifestyle, this is much more important than achieving the elusive $1,000,000 mark. In and of itself, becoming a millionaire does not necessarily equate with true prosperity.

You like your job, your asset accrual is solid, and we assume that your living expenses are satisfied without excessive debt. It does appear that you are clearly on the right path.

As we stated in the beginning of chapter 1, some behavior modification will be required on your journey to reach prosperity. Even when all is seemingly going well, we must be receptive to reassessing opportunities that are hiding in plain sight.

What are your goals for wealth building? What will you do differently to reach your goals? A self-audit checklist shown in Table 2-4 is an appropriate tool to assess your current financial status.

Table 2-4
Self-Audit Checklist

- ☐ What is the value of my financial assets?
- ☐ What is the current market value of my prime residence?
- ☐ What is the current market value of my other real estate?
- ☐ What is the value of all other assets that I own?
- ☐ How much debt do I have?
- ☐ What is my net worth?
- ☐ What is in my value system?
- ☐ Do I take sufficient time to carefully consider my life choices?
- ☐ Am I saving/investing enough?
- ☐ Am I on the right track for wealth building?
- ☐ What is my total household income?
- ☐ What is the balance of my emergency fund?
- ☐ How much disposable income do I have?
- ☐ Do I need help with financial planning?
- ☐ Am I proactive toward debt reduction?
- ☐ Do I avoid impulse buying?
- ☐ If debt reduction is effective, what will I do with the extra money?
- ☐ Have I prepared a well-grounded budget?
- ☐ Do I have a will, estate plan, health care proxy and/or living will?
- ☐ Do I have a viable contingency plan in the event of job loss?
- ☐ Do I have a structured retirement plan?
- ☐ What is my action plan to achieve my goals?

When true opportunity knocks, be sure to be amenable.

Getting Personal

Dear Drs. WDD and RVN,

I am twenty-seven years old and work as an engineer at a microchip manufacturer. The pay and benefits are good. Our primary retirement plan is fully paid by our employer and is based on 15 percent of our pay. Also, we have an optional supplemental plan that the company will match up to $3,500 per year. I can only afford to put $1,000 into this plan, but I feel good that I am saving for the future and will be able to afford the good life during retirement.

Do you think I am on track to become rich?

Chipping Away

Dear Chipping,

Yes! You are on the right track.

Of course, a big question is, how controlled are your expenses? In terms of accruing more wealth, you are foregoing an opportunity to accrue $5,000 ($2,500 + matching $2,500) each year by not maxing out the company's generous offer of funding your supplemental plan in part. Consider this: if you miss this tax-deferred offer just over a twenty-year period with a return of 6 percent per year, you are missing out on an additional accrual of $194,964. Even when considering the effects of inflation, it significantly contributes to wealth building. Further, the results would be dramatically better if the timeline went from twenty years to forty years (full retirement age).

Do something to secure this offer: cut your living expenses, work some overtime, get some spousal help, maybe take a part-time job, if practical. Just think, when you put one dollar into this account you receive an immediate return of 100 percent.

WEALTH IN PERSPECTIVE

Consider the varied perspectives about wealth from several publicly documented vignettes. Some of these people clearly know what it means to be richer than a millionaire, and, in our view, some, sadly, can never have enough.

- *Richer than a millionaire:* Carol Hochberg died at the age of forty. An Ivy-educated (Penn and Harvard) advocate for victims of breast cancer, she quit her job as an investment banker "with a six-figure salary and a substantial personal portfolio" after she was diagnosed with the disease, concluding that there was "more to life than making rich men richer." After her cancer diagnosis in 1995, she said: "I was waiting for something to be committed and enthusiastic about. I guess I took cancer as a sign." For the last three years of her life, she ably used her skills to help others through relentless advocacy and lobbying.[38]

- *Richer than a millionaire:* Thomas S. Monaghan sold more than 90 percent of the closely held Domino's Pizza he founded for $1 billion to Bain Capital, so that he could work on his charitable foundation. In recent years, Mr. Monaghan renounced and sold many of his material distractions, including the Detroit Tigers baseball team, his helicopter, his plane, and his yacht.[39]

- *Not richer than a millionaire:* Roy Raymond—an entrepreneur—lived from 1946–1993. He earned a Stanford MBA in 1971 and founded Victoria's Secret in 1977. In 1982 he sold Victoria's Secret to the Limited, Inc., for $2 million and yet was forced to file for bankruptcy protection in 1986, losing an elegant Victorian home, two cars, and a vacation home near Lake Tahoe. He had a thirst for achievement: "There was no reason he needed to work again…" but "that would have been very hard for him," said Gaye Raymond, Roy's ex-wife since 1990. Mr. Raymond apparently leapt off the Golden Gate Bridge at the age of forty-seven after "failure to regain glory."[40]

- *Not richer than a millionaire:* Richard Cory—a poem by Edwin Arlington Robinson[41]—was popularized by the singing duo Simon and Garfunkel in the 1960s. Richard Cory was well-off, well connected, and envied by many. So the song goes: he had "power, grace and style…he surely must be happy with everything he's got…he freely gave to charity…so my mind was filled with wonder when…Richard Cory went home last night and put a bullet through his head."

While we can only speculate about Richard Cory, he would probably be listed as a well-satisfied millionaire. We just don't know what his anxiety level was, but we would suspect it was high, as he apparently had nothing to live for. This is despite the admiration he received and outward gifts he made to charity. Who would have predicted the outcome? Obviously, there is always the question of psychological balance and a variety of life-threatening addictions.

As the next section summarizes, it is a challenge to become a millionaire. But even if millionaire status is attained, there is no guarantee that satisfaction will follow.

HOW MANY MILLIONAIRES ARE THERE? IT DEPENDS.

A 2013 survey by the Federal Reserve[42] of the 122,500,000 "families"[43] in the United States shows that the median net worth was $81,200. This value includes both financial and nonfinancial assets. The top 10 percent, namely 12,250,000 families, had at a minimum, a net worth of $941,700. For these top 10 percent, the median net worth was $1,871,800, and the mean value was $4,024,800. Table 2-5 summarizes net worth based on Federal Reserve data.

Table 2-5
Financial Net Worth of 122,500,000 US Families

Percentile	Minimum for Lower End of Category	Median	Mean	Number of US Families
Less than 25	(negative)		-$13,400	30,625,000
25 to 49.9	$8,800	$31,300	$35,900	30,625,000
50 to 74.9	$81,200	$168,100	$177,700	30,625,000
75 to 89.9	$317,300	$505,800	$546,200	18,375,000
90 to 100	$941,700	$1,871,800	$4,024,800	12,250,000

Using proprietary methods, multiple organizations[44] provided estimates of millionaire households as of 2014, as shown in Table 2-6. In sum, it truly depends on which assets are included in the calculation of household net worth. The most restrictive calculation suggests 3.5 percent or 1/25 of households are millionaires; the most liberal suggests 11.6 percent or 3/25 are millionaire households. Indeed, the estimate made by Credit Suisse seems most consistent with that of the Federal Reserve. Nevertheless, all of the measures show that the number of households in the millionaire category is in the minority.

Table 2-6
Number of Millionaire Households
Based on Various Assumptions

Organization	Number of Millionaire Households
Capgemini & RBC Wealth Management *(investible assets only)*	4,300,000
Boston Consulting Group *(excluding RE, collectibles, luxury goods)*	6,900,000
Spectrem Group *(excluding primary residence)*	10,100,000
Credit Suisse *(including all assets)*	14,200,000

Fortunately, the vast majority of US households are happy or satisfied with their lots in life, irrespective of their financial net worth, with 88 percent of the US adult population indicating that they are "pretty happy" or "very happy."[45] To keep this in perspective, according to an instructor in the department of psychiatry at Harvard Medical School, the probability of finding a US household headed up by a sociopath is, thankfully, only one in twenty-five.[46]

Clearly, being richer than a millionaire takes more than money. Chapter 3 examines the inflow and outflow of earnings at a national level and serves as a basis of comparison for individuals.

MONEY IN AND MONEY OUT

MONEY IN

In *The Millionaire Next Door*, the focus was on net worth, not income. If one had twice the expected net worth, one would be designated a prodigious accumulator of wealth (PAW), and if the net worth was one half of what was expected, one would be designated an under accumulator of wealth (UAW). One cannot build net worth until the discipline to save more and consume less becomes ingrained. We also find in our research that those who do achieve millionaire status report that they save about 20 percent of their income annually.

Do you spend more than you earn? If so, financial prosperity is not a likely outcome. Figure 3-1 summarizes a study of economic well-being by the board of governors of the Federal Reserve System.[47] It reveals that for all households, 41 percent of the population spends less than their income. Thus, this segment has funds available for saving or investing. However, 37 percent of households have spending equal to income, and 20 percent say that spending is greater than their income.

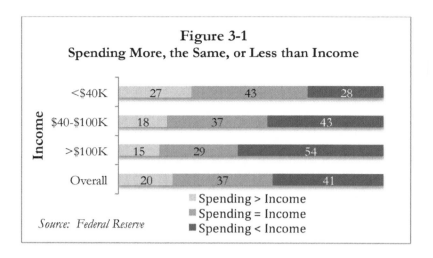

Figure 3-1
Spending More, the Same, or Less than Income

Source: Federal Reserve

Households with less than $40,000 income have the highest level of debt dependency, with twenty seven percent spending more than they make. This may be an obvious assessment, but it further indicates a devastating downward financial spiral. How will members of these households reverse their plight? What is your income, and is there enough to allocate for saving or investing? Perhaps a personal strengths, weaknesses, opportunities, and threats (SWOT) analysis is needed. This is further discussed later in this chapter.

Clearly, higher income levels help facilitate wealth accrual but do not guarantee it, since 15 percent of those with incomes of over $100,000 spend more than they earn, and 29 percent spend all of their earnings.

Another question asked in the aforementioned study was, of those who saved, what percent was set aside for retirement and for other purposes?

Overall, the majority (57.1 percent) save for retirement. However, this figure varies by income. About a third (37.4 percent) of the households earning less than $40,000 save for retirement. About half (54.2 percent) of middle-income earners save for retirement. But nearly three quarters (70.1 percent) of those with incomes of $100,000 or more save for retirement. That is a good example of forward thinking, by not allowing expenses to overtake your income.

According to the Federal Reserve[48] there is some good and bad news in regard to family finances. As a result of improvements in economic activity and rising house and corporate equity values, there have been increases in average and median family net worth between 2013 and 2016. Between 2013 and 2016, median family income increased 10 percent while mean family income grew 14 percent. In 2016, families at the high end of income and wealth distributions had large gains in mean and median net worth.

Retirement plan participation and retirement account asset values rose between 2013 and 2016 for families across the income distribution, with the largest proportional increases in participation occurring among families in the bottom half of the income distribution.

Families at the low end of income and wealth distribution had large gains in mean and median net worth after past declines between 2010 and 2013.

Unfortunately, in 2016, still 15 percent of families reported that they were spending more than their income. Those in this category covered their shortfalls by drawing from savings or investments (44 percent) and borrowing, including use of credit cards (43 percent). Other options were to get help from others, part-time work, and negotiating payments.

Nearly all age groups experienced increases in median net worth between 2013 and 2016, with the exception of families between ages 65 and 74. This group experienced a modest decline.

Mean net worth grew for about 50 percent of the age groups. However, families under 45 and families between ages 65 and 74 experienced declines in mean net worth between 2013 and 2016.

The largest gains in both median and mean net worth occurred among the oldest families ages 75 plus, who experienced a 32 percent increase in median net worth and a 60 percent increase in mean net worth.

These patterns by age group were generally the opposite of the 2010–13 period, when mean and median net worth increased for families under age 45, decreased for those between ages 45 and 64, increased for those between ages 65 and 74, and decreased for the oldest group.

MONEY OUT

Now, let's look at how incomes are spent. Table 3-1 illustrates how income is redistributed into multiple markets.

Table 3-1
How Americans Spent Their Money
in 2015

Spending	Amount
Housing	22.7%
Life insurance & pensions	11.3%
Health care	7.8%
Groceries	7.2%
Cars & trucks	7.1%
Utilities	6.9%
Transportation	6.1%
Eating out	5.4%
Entertainment	5.1%
Miscellaneous	4.5%
Gas	3.7%
Clothing	3.3%
Home furnishings	3.3%
Charity, alimony	3.3%
Education	2.4%

Source: Bureau of Labor Statistics

Not surprisingly, housing takes the biggest bite out of our income, which is followed with life insurance and pensions. Currently, health care is the wild card in the arena of spending our dollars. Estimates for health care coverage are generally increasing, for some states by double digits. According to *Forbes*, US health care costs do in fact rise faster than rates of inflation, and the forecasts for the future are alarming.[49]

The Centers for Medicare and Medicaid Services report that for the years of 2015 through 2025, health care spending will grow an average rate of 5.8 percent per year. Health care costs are expected to grow 1.3 percent faster than the GDP. Consequently, the cost of health care is forecast to rise to 20.1 percent of the GDP by 2025. Prescription drug costs are projected to grow on average 6.7 percent per year through 2025.[50]

However, these reports look tame compared with other forecasts that reveal a shockingly dire outcome with health care rate hikes. A *Wall Street Journal* report states that premiums for the Affordable Care Act's benchmark health plans will have an average increase in premiums of 25 percent in 2017.[51] Some states will increase even more. What this means to household budgets is that such increases will now require much more of the family's expenditures. Keep in mind that in 2014, health care costs were 8 percent of household expenses.[52]

As we can see, a lot of our disposable income is spent on necessities such as housing and health care costs. Financial planning is increasingly important. Clearly identify your discretionary income and closely monitor it for saving or investing. Millionaires are vigilant about spending.

Getting Personal

Dear Drs. WDD and RVN,

I can't help myself; I keep buying stuff. "On sale" triggers something inside of me to rush in for the bargains. My closets are full of dresses, sweaters, business apparel, shoes, and ironically, pocket books.

I know I am impulsive, and this trait impacts my ability to save. I earn enough to excessively spend, but I know my wealth accumulation suffers.

I'd really like to be financially secure, and I know I need a drain plug. Could you offer a simple solution to help get over this fatal attraction to spending?

Debbie in Debt

Dear Debbie,

Not so sure about a simple solution, but some thoughts follow. First of all, it is good that you recognize that your impulsive spending behavior impacts wealth accumulation.

Think of yourself as a victim of "hot-button triggers." Marketers are skilled professionals who know how to target their desired markets. We are all targets! They are after all of our income. Superficial spending is a decadent habit that needs breaking.

Recognize the real differences between needs and wants. Do you really need another sweater, or is it so attractive (especially on sale) that you just want it? Ask yourself: Need or want? The latest hot brand name is just a promotional ploy to appeal to your need of self-esteem. Don't subscribe to, "I am what I wear" or that conspicuous consumption is cool. From a marketer's point of view such believers are ideal targets. Don't allow yourself to be manipulated. Your drain plug, in a word, is *abstain*!

PERSONAL VALUES

Wealth accumulation is largely attitudinal. What really matters to you? Is becoming a millionaire a worthwhile endeavor? How are your values ranked? If wealth status is a worthy goal, it must be congruent with the components within your value system. So what's in your value system? Consider the factors presented in Table 3-2, which are listed in alphabetical order.

Table 3-2
Non-exhaustive Listing of Values

Accomplishment	Expertise	Leisure	Wealth
Acknowledgment	Family	Pleasure	
Autonomy	Friendship	Recognition	
Belief	Happiness	Religion	
Challenge	Health	Spirituality	
Cooperation	Honesty	Variety	
Creativity	Intimacy	Wardrobe	

Refer to the above-listed motivators and rank them one through twenty-two. This will prove difficult, but such an exercise may help you to better understand your perspective and how it influences most of the decisions you make. What you value is what you believe you need in life to feel satisfied.[53]

Vignette: Job Mismatch

Jack M., twenty-four years old, interviewed for a job and sold himself as a very hard worker with high energy levels and no problem with working overtime (overtime requirements were stated as an essential criterion for the job). He was hired, and all was well until after he married and had a child. The required schedule of working extra hours during evenings and on weekends, although rewarded with a large paycheck, was no longer so attractive to him. His job performance slipped.

Jack's value system changed. He was in the wrong job.

Jack was able to find another job that had a smaller but sufficient base pay, and importantly, it did not require overtime work.

Accelerated wealth accumulation was not as important to Jack as was family time together.

THE EVIL APPEAL OF DEBT

An impediment to wealth building is immediate gratification. The power that marketers wield over consumers results in persuasive impulses to spend beyond our means. Such unwarranted purchases are enabled through the use of credit and/or debit cards. Immediate gratification, as a burning desire driven by our value system, may have a feel-good interlude, but the downside is recognition that more debt has been created.

A long-term overview of household debt to disposable personal income points out a relatively short-lived trend of debt reduction in 2008. The most likely cause was the result of difficult economic times.[54]

Household debt includes the home mortgage and consumer credit, which consists of credit card liabilities, student loans, and car loans. Overall, household debt increased from 1954 until 2008 and then declined. In 2013, household debt began to rise again.[55]

All things considered, consumer spending is still the engine driving economic growth and will always be encouraged by marketers. Personal consumption is nearly 70 percent of the GDP. Conversely, savings rates are relatively nominal. Some will save, and others will spend beyond their means, resulting in an accumulation of debt that reduces or eliminates the possibility of financial independence.

CONTROLLING DEBT

As revealed earlier, higher incomes certainly help with debt avoidance, and higher incomes correlate with higher education. In 2015 the US

Bureau of Labor Statistics reported that the median earnings for high school graduates were $35,256, and for college graduates with a bachelor's degree, the median earnings were $59,124.

A strengths, weaknesses, opportunities, and threats (SWOT) analysis may be an appropriate exercise for anyone having difficulty reaching his or her potential for higher income.

SWOT ANALYSIS

Essentially, this analysis is a self-assessment of where you are. As objectively as possible, identify your strengths, weaknesses, opportunities, and threats as related to your career. The examples used in the SWOT analysis are based on a compilation of recommendations from the book *Life after Layoff*.[56]

A non-exhaustive checklist format of examples (in random order) for your SWOT analysis follows. Be brutally honest with yourself.

Strengths (Some examples)
□ You have demonstrated problem solving skills.
□ Your credentials/education requirements for your job are current.
□ You have demonstrated leadership skills.
□ You have solid sources for networking.
□ You have appropriate professional/trade memberships.
□ You have major achievements in your work history.
□ Your values are compatible with the organization for whom you work.
□ Others?

Weaknesses (Some examples)
□ You lack appropriate education/training for promotion.
□ Your level of experience is insufficient for a promotion.
□ Your college degree is obsolete.
□ You are not able/willing to geographically relocate.

☐ You are not perceived by your colleagues as a team player.

☐ Others?

Opportunities (Some examples)

☐ You have training opportunities provided by your company.

☐ You have company support to stay technologically current.

☐ You stay informed about ongoing current events, especially as related to your industry and the economy.

☐ You are in a growing industry.

☐ You are a candidate for a headhunter search.

☐ You have meaningful contacts within your industry who are supportive of you.

☐ You attend your industry-related conferences.

☐ Others?

Threats (Some examples)

☐ You are in a declining industry.

☐ Your company is considering a merger or a buyout, which could lead to redundant workers.

☐ Layoffs are pending.

☐ A demotion is likely.

☐ You have minimal academic/professional/trade credentials.

☐ You are not current with forthcoming changes in technology as related to your career.

☐ Others?

Your personal SWOT analysis provides an overview of your current self-assessment. Recognize that you have freewill, and you have the option to make choices that will increase your chances to reach prosperity. Build on your strengths, shore up your weaknesses, recognize opportunities, and prepare for threats (these will always exist).

Be aware of your SWOT assessment and your value system. Sometimes opportunity presents itself, but because of an accustomed steady-state lifestyle, good fortune possibilities are missed.

Vignette: Early Notification

A large manufacturing plant was closing and relocating. Employees were given eighteen months notification. They had to decide if they wanted to move their families to the new location. There was no promise of the same job, only that they would be hired if they chose to stay on. Predictably, many started looking for jobs locally. With many two-career families, moving was a problem for most. Others just made no plans and were willing to wait and see what happened. One of the managers, who had been with the company for twenty years, decided this might be a time for all kinds of changes. A new place to live sounded exciting. His wife was self-employed and believed that she might have more advantages in the new and larger city.

The company was just beginning their International Organization for Standardization (ISO) program. With his management and engineering background and his seniority, this particular manager volunteered to work with the new ISO project. It would require that he travel weekly to the new location, working with staff in both plants. Although it sounded hectic initially, he was able to check on real estate options, look at a variety of neighborhoods, and find out some information about his wife's options. All this information was gathered long before the move. As a consequence, he was able to locate housing at a good price, before all the other relocated employees moved to the area in search of scarce housing. He and his wife actually felt somewhat settled in their new home shortly after the move because of the earlier preparations.

He became a much more valuable employee and received a large increase in pay. Further, he was able to enrich his own career with new work and challenges. He was integrated into the new team before he had to move. There were many tangible as well as intangible benefits with his choice to move in a new direction. In addition, he had a chance to introduce himself to the new environment.

Awareness of forthcoming change can be a gift, if exploited properly. Threats converted into opportunities provide an excellent turnaround.

ACTIONS TO CONSIDER

A secure, appropriate, and well-paying job is key to wealth building and well-being. Of course, in addition to an appropriate job, there are proactive and practical measures that may be taken to ensure progress toward prosperity. Some suggested courses of action follow.

- *Immediately* start accumulating cash through automatic savings from your paycheck to your bank account.

- Build a sufficient amount of funds for diversified investments, and then acquire your choice of savings, stocks, bonds, or other assets.

- Write and use a budget. Get rid of recurring expenses wherever possible, such as credit card payments. Be extremely cautious about incurring credit card debt. Think of your credit cards as potential instruments of evil.

- Be sure that you are taking full advantage of employer-offered matching retirement fund contributions. Set up a supplemental tax-deferred retirement account.

- Always live below your means.

- Ignore the mantra used by retailers: "The more you spend, the more you save."

- Remember: the most appropriate education pays big dividends.

- Don't fall prey to temptation to keep up with the Joneses. Conspicuous consumption stagnates wealth building.

Clearly, we all have different perspectives that are formed on the basis of our individual value systems.

Let's move on to chapter 4. This chapter summarizes what has been long known about the way to wealth, and some of the best practices to reach it.

CHAPTER 4

THE WAY TO WEALTH

One needs to balance financial well-being with happiness and good health for true prosperity. While it is beneficial to have all three, in our view, happiness and good health trump financial well-being. Two centuries ago, English writer and clergyman Charles Caleb Colton (1780 – 1832) eloquently wrote: "It is only when the rich are sick that they fully feel the impotence of wealth." We know of no one who would argue with that. With good health and motivation, everybody has the ability to generate financial wealth.

In the next chapter we address happiness in more detail. Of course, wealth does not guarantee happiness. This truth has been know for at least 2,000 years, as revealed in an observation by the Roman Empire historian Publius Cornelius Tacitus (56 – 120): "We see many who are struggling against adversity who are happy, and more although abounding in wealth, who are wretched." But for now, let's focus on the way to financial wealth.

Numerous resources provide advice about building wealth.[57] Knight Kiplinger, then editor-in-chief of *Kiplinger's Personal Finance Magazine*, gives some of the best, and he does it all with just eight pieces of advice.[58] However, even his advice echoes the wisdom of Benjamin Franklin. Discipline is the key. Recall Benjamin Franklin's conclusion that ninety percent of your success depends on your willingness to succeed. *The Millionaire Next Door* emphasized this exact point: success in wealth building requires personal discipline. You can read all the books published on personal finance and wealth building, but if you don't implement the advice it will just be an interesting academic exercise.

Let us now summarize what is known about wealth formation, and then examine a framework to understand the difference between your needs and your wants.

A RECAP OF ADVICE FROM BENJAMIN FRANKLIN

1. **Be industrious** (industry gives comfort, and plenty, and respect).
2. **Persevere** (there are no gains without pains).
3. **Practice good stewardship** (oversee your own affairs with your own eyes).
4. **Be frugal** (it is easier to suppress the first desire than to satisfy all that follow it).
5. **Avoid debt** (think what you do when you run in debt; you give to another power over your liberty).
6. **Be humble** (do not depend too much upon your own industry, and frugality, and prudence, though excellent things; for they may all be blasted, without the blessing of Heaven; and, therefore, ask the blessing humbly).
7. **Be charitable** (be not uncharitable to those that at present seem to want it, but comfort and help them).

These seven principles proposed by Franklin were augmented by a Rand study on wealth from 1995. In reviewing that study, a *New York Times* reporter began with the following analysis: "Benjamin Franklin and your mother may have been right after all, at least according to a new [Rand] study: affluent Americans typically got that way by staying healthy, getting married and working hard for a good wage, rather than by inheriting their money."[59]

The authors reason that marriage encourages people to save more, and people who are healthy can work longer and don't spend as much on medical bills.

An economic analysis of health and wealth supports the Rand study. It finds that "men in the United States with family incomes in the top 5 percent of the distribution in 1980 had about 25 percent longer to live than did those in the bottom 5 percent."[60] Clearly, the longer one lives, the greater opportunity for compound interest and returns on investments.

In an analysis of death certificates, the National Center for Health Statistics finds that those who were married at time of death had the greatest longevity. Those who were divorced lived the least long. Details are shown in Table 4-1.

Table 4-1
Age at Time of Death
(for those who lived to at least 50)

Marital Status	Men	Women
Married	77.6	81.0
Never Married	69.2	77.4
Divorced	67.1	72.0

Source: National Center for Health Statistics

MARRIAGE, SEX, AND HAPPINESS

Marriage is almost an essential prerequisite for wealth building. The late sociologist James Q. Wilson found that "married people are happier than unmarried ones of the same age, not only in the United States, but in at least seventeen other countries where similar inquiries have been made. And there seems to be good reasons for that happiness. People who are married not only have higher incomes and enjoy greater emotional support, they tend to be healthier. Married people live longer than unmarried ones, not only in the United States but abroad."[61] Perhaps not surprisingly, a University of Chicago sociologist concluded that divorce can be hazardous to your health. At the ninth annual Smart Marriages conference, Professor Linda Waite updated her analysis on 8,600 people between fifty-one and sixty-one.[62] In a news report about her findings, she concludes: "Divorce or widowhood creates stress, which is associated with chronic health problems...a happy marriage offers about the same health benefits as an undisrupted one."[63]

These health benefits of an intact marriage extend to the children in the household, as well. In an analysis of the 2002 National Survey of America's Families by the private research group Child Trends, the implications are clear. For example, of twelve- to seventeen-year-olds from single-parent or cohabitating-parents households, 23 percent were suspended from school in the past year. In contrast, just 10 percent of the same-age children from married parents households were suspended. Similarly, children from married parents households were twice as likely to be healthy than those from single parents or cohabitating parents households.[64]

By analyzing sixteen thousand surveys from adults who participated in the General Social Surveys of the United States from 1988 through 2002, two economists[65] found, contrary to popular wisdom, that money does indeed buy more happiness. They also found that married people have more sex than those who are single, divorced, widowed, or separated. Further, they found that sexual activity enters strongly positive in happiness equations. In an interview[66] about the study, the authors provided some background information not found in the final paper. The two key findings were that marriage provides $100,000 worth of happiness annually, and divorce takes an annual emotional toll of $66,000.

A conclusion consistent with this study is found in a Rand report that examined marriage, assets, and savings: "Married couples apparently save significantly more than other households. If marriage is related to household savings, the sharp decline in the number of American households who are married may be part of the reason for the secular fall in US private savings rates. For households that remain married, the duration of the marriage positively affects wealth beyond the simple age-wealth relationship. On the other hand, for households that remain divorced or separated, the duration of this situation negatively affects wealth." [67]

While it might seem odd to assign monetary values to personal relationships, the positive (marriage) and negative (divorce) directions suggested are consistent in both the economic and the psychology literatures. And it is consistent with our legal system, as revealed by the remark made during an interview with a millionaire who insisted on anonymity: "I can't afford a divorce." This speaks volumes.

So what happens when the relationship fails? Consider the plight of lonesome George.

Getting Personal

Dear Drs. WDD and RVN,

My wife, "Sweet Sara," gave me the boot. She made a big scene, threw my stuff in a pile, called me many unkind names, and said, "Get out!" Wow! I never saw it coming. Anyhow, not sure what to do now. We lived off my salary, and she saved all of hers. I was OK with that because I thought we'd be together forever.

I am thirty-seven years old, and I have a good-paying, secure job. I have never been a saver because of my lifestyle. I know I must make changes and now recognize that I don't want to live as I did with not-so-sweet Sara.

Any guidance would help.
Lonesome George

Dear George,

You didn't say why Sweet Sara gave you the boot. Maybe it was justified?

Obviously, some legal matters are forthcoming, but to go to your question of guidance: you have to create a budget. List all of your living costs and subtract that total from your net income.

You said that you are not a saver, but does your employer contribute to a company-sponsored retirement plan? Is there a matching-contribution offer? Will you have any extra money from your paycheck after paying your bills? If so, this is called discretionary income, which means you can save it or spend it. Of course, your lifestyle guides your spending habits. Maybe there is room for tightening the financial belt.

Hopefully, reconciliation is a possibility rather than the alternative.

SUPPORTING STUDIES OF PROFILES OF THE WEALTHY

Elements of three contemporary studies corroborate the Rand and Franklin findings.

- "Who becomes wealthy? Usually the wealthy individual is a businessman who has lived in the same town for all his adult life. This person owns a small factory, a chain of stores, or a service company. He has married once and remains married. He lives next door to people with a fraction of his wealth. He is a compulsive saver and investor. And he has made his money on his own."[68]

- Successful MBA graduates are more likely to be entrepreneurial with a competitive drive and a desire to win. In a twenty-year longitudinal analysis of the class of '74 Harvard MBAs, the average income and sense of power and autonomy were nearly twice as large for "entrepreneurs, small business people, and non-manufacturers" than for "professional managers, medium and large business people, and manufacturers." Interestingly, those with lower GMAT scores (a test taken for graduate school admission) earn approximately 25 percent more than those with higher scores (perhaps because they unknowingly take more risk and therefore enjoy greater rewards). There was no correlation between parental net worth and the graduates' incomes, nor was there a relationship between the graduates' intelligence and incomes.[69]

- Family financial net worth is about five times greater, on average, for the self-employed versus those working for someone else.[70]

Self-employment is, for many, the American dream. Set your own hours, take a vacation, and maybe give yourself a raise—you decide. No time card and no meddling boss. No layoffs to worry about and best of all you keep the profits. Be an entrepreneur—it's not a job; it's a venture.

All things considered, self-employment has many attractions, but there are countless pitfalls associated with working for oneself. Unfortunately, the success rate for business start-ups is not encouraging. However, there will always be individuals who have an entrepreneurial drive and will start a business. Self-employment is further discussed in chapter 6, in the context of entrepreneurship.

Whether self-employed or not, the meanings of prosperity will vary from one person's perspective to another's. However, viewing the concept of prosperity as a compilation of key life factors offers a framework for consideration. We are driven to satisfy basic needs, and our motivation is contingent on the level and urgency of need. Yet it is not uncommon to confuse needs with wants.

MOTIVATION

One practical way to assess self-motivation and resulting behavior is to refer to Abraham Maslow's Hierarchy of Needs,[71] which serves as a means to differentiate between needs and wants. This model is shown in Figure 4-1.

Figure 4-1

Maslow's Hierarchy of Needs

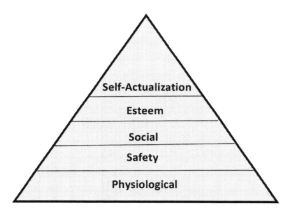

The extent to which these needs are met will vary contingent upon one's environmental circumstances. Cultural factors, socioeconomic conditions, socialism, and capitalism drive quality of life.[72]

At the most basic level, a person's needs are sustenance, water, some form of shelter, air, elimination, sleep, and sex for procreation. All creatures have these basic needs. However, humans living in industrialized nations experience frequent confusion between needs and wants.

Consequently, wants are perceived as needs. If given a choice, who would opt for basic nourishment over a fine meal?

Marketers, through the use of traditional forms of promotion and state-of-the-art social media, bombard us with messages of persuasion that wants are our essential needs.

Every day we make choices related to food consumption on whether to eat at home or dine out. Of course, dining in or out will satisfy the need for food and likely a whole lot more. The kitchen table provides not only a place for meal consumption but also a gathering place for family and/or friends to socially interact. The same may be said of dining out in a restaurant. Trends derived by the Economic Research Service of the US Department of Agriculture indicate that even in tight economic times, restaurants and their food and beverage services are a quite popular way to meet basic needs along with opportunities for socializing. However, there are disparities based on income, as shown in Figure 4-2. Households in the lowest income quintile spent one third (34 percent) of their food budget for food away from home, and households in the top quintile spent more than half (51 percent) for food away from home.[73]

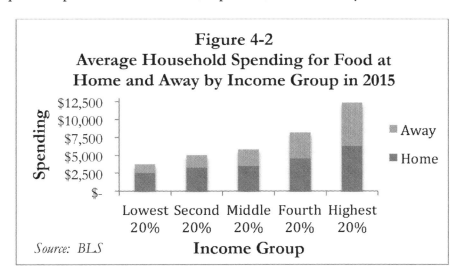

Figure 4-2
Average Household Spending for Food at Home and Away by Income Group in 2015

Source: BLS

Additionally, while water is a basic need, how it's met—bottled water versus tap water, for example—can almost turn bottled water into a need.

Consumers are quite willing to purchase bottled water as an alternative to drinking from the tap. The Beverage Marketing Corporation[74] reported in 2016 that thirty-six gallons of bottled water are consumed per person per year. Of course, it is true that there are times when local water supplies are deemed unfit for consumption; such circumstances would be a valid reason to make a choice to purchase bottled water.

But generally, wants dominate needs—and within reason, this does not have to be a bad thing. There are many products and services that will offer the promise of exceptional satisfaction to fill the most basic needs.

The point of illustrating the deliberate confusion of needs and wants is that we are often led into temptation to purchase items that offer more than just satisfaction of basic needs. Sometimes it may be just an iconic brand mark or name that helps us justify paying a much higher price. Would a less expensive substitute product satisfy the need? Of course, choosing a less expensive product will enable you to retain more disposable and/or discretionary income.

Do premium purchases make us happy? Or would having more cash for other uses (including saving) make us happier? A state of happiness is a desirable place to be. As Benjamin Franklin points out, "The Constitution only guarantees the American people the right to pursue happiness. You have to catch it yourself." Maslow states that happiness is found when one is self-actualized, becoming all you care to be.[75] The journey to reach self-actualization may be a bumpy ride that requires steadfastness.

Getting Personal

Dear Drs. WDD and RVN,

I know I spend too much when shopping. It is my weakness. Ironically, at first it makes me feel good, and then these pleasant feelings shift to those of guilt.

I seem to be wired to search for happiness through acquiring more and more stuff. On the other hand, I wind up donating much of my stuff to charitable organizations, which makes me feel both good and bad—good because I'm helping others and bad because I over spent, again.

Your insight and advice will be truly appreciated.

Regards,
Gina Giver

Dear Gina,

You have acknowledged that you have a problem with over-spending, and that is a good beginning. We are bombarded with constant invitations to spend our money. Advertisements are everywhere—TV, radio, Internet, magazines, newspapers, bill-boards, flyers, all forms of social media—my gosh! Temptation is everywhere! Wow, we are all invited to become spendaholics. All of us are marketers' targets. Think about it.

How will you accrue wealth if you spend yourself into oblivion? Also, your feelings of happiness are fleeting, as you acknowledge. Sort out your real needs from the excesses promoted by the temptation fabricators.

Giving away your superfluous stuff is a further sign that you regret your excessive buying. Focus on what you truly need, and reject all other appeals to open your purse.

Your feelings of guilt will dissipate, and the money that you are not spending will serve as the needed building blocks for wealth accumulation. Now *that* is something that will give you genuine and lasting good feelings.

Let's move on to the next level: safety needs. Sure, we have a need to be free from physical and psychological harm. Yes, there are many threats within our contemporary environment. We are reminded in all forms of the media to be vigilant at all times. Of course, that is a good starting point. However, being aware of one's surroundings may not be enough. There are many environmental factors, including where you are, when you are there, and what you are doing at a given time. The wrong time and the wrong place can be a bad mix.

After two years of decline, the estimated number of violent crimes in the nation increased 3.9 percent in 2015 when compared with 2014 data, according to FBI figures, which follow.[76]

- In 2015, there were an estimated 1,197,704 violent crimes. Murder and non-negligent manslaughter increased 10.8 percent when compared with estimates from 2014.

- Rape and aggravated assault increased 6.3 percent and 4.6 percent, respectively, while robbery increased 1.4 percent.

- Nationwide, there were an estimated 7,993,631 property crimes. The estimated numbers for two of the three property crimes show declines when compared with the previous year's estimates. Burglaries dropped 7.8 percent, and larceny-thefts declined 1.8 percent, but motor vehicle thefts rose 3.1 percent.

- Collectively, victims of property crimes (excluding arson) suffered losses estimated at $14.3 billion in 2015.

Safety concerns relate to almost everything in life. Marketers are readily available to offer solutions for every concern. It is up to the consumer to decide on the most appropriate balance of need and want.

Other safety issues relate to an individual's risk tolerance. Some people have a higher risk tolerance for certain activities. For example, a young person is more likely to invest with a desire for a high rate of return, whereas someone nearing retirement is likely to be risk averse, thus choosing a more conservative approach to investing. Assuming all is congruent with life expectancy statistics, this is the best choice, if for no other reason than the older investor does not have as many years left to recover from any losses with investments. Just for the record, according to the National Center for Health Statistics, life expectancy is 78.8 years.[77]

The next level of needs is social. Most of us are social beings and thus require some amount of interaction with others. The possibilities of fulfilling these needs are almost limitless. From the dinner table at home to international travel, only imagination and financial resources impose limiting boundaries. Some join country clubs; others volunteer their time and support to nonprofit organizations. Some do both. Maslow does state that being helpful to others will contribute to the overall feeling of intrinsic happiness. [78]

Getting Personal

Dear Drs. WDD and RVN,

I am blessed in every way—a great family, a good-paying job that I enjoy, and good health for my entire family.

    I've been thinking about volunteering for a nonprofit organization on a limited basis. My question about volunteering is, does helping others provide a more feel-good benefit to the volunteer than actual benefit to those being helped?

Unsure Annie

Dear Annie,

Volunteering most likely will do both. It will help the volunteer at an intrinsic level and help the recipient at a practical level. It largely depends on what you volunteer for and the extent to which you complete your tasks.

    Working with others for the benefit of the less fortunate provides an opportunity for camaraderie, a feeling of accomplishment, and in all likelihood will enhance one's self-esteem. Further, volunteering is a chance for hands-on networking and a good feature on one's resume.

    So yes, offering one's time and talent is a choice that helps others and clearly yields potential benefits to the volunteer.

Moving upward on the hierarchy, we find esteem needs. This includes both esteem from others and self-esteem. Are you satisfied? Do you like yourself? If you don't, it is probably going to be difficult for others to disagree with your opinion.

Your ideal self may be in conflict with your mirror image. Some tend to match product images with self-image, and others are susceptible to matching portrayed product images with ideal-self perceptions.[79] Motivation to align your real self with your ideal self may be triggered.

Assuming an acceptable balance within the hierarchy of needs through the esteem level, it is appropriate to move to the apex: self-actualization. Be all you care to be. Hopefully, a sense of internal peace accompanies this achievement. And hopefully, it will last. Life is full of fleeting moments of happiness. Maslow put forth the idea of self-transcendence, which manifests itself through helping others in need and a resulting intrinsic happiness.[80] There are no guarantees for ascension to or permanence of this elevated status.

Vignette: Natalie Inside the Pyramid

Natalie T. is a forty-nine-year-old professor of management. She holds a PhD, is tenured, earns $92,000 a year, and has a generous benefits package. She has been employed by the same university for the past seven years. Natalie enjoys teaching and does not feel overly burdened by expectations of publishing papers.

Dr. T.'s balance sheet reveals a net worth of nearly one million dollars. She is frugal, has a generous retirement plan, and makes supplemental retirement account contributions. The retirement plan forecast is an accumulation of $1.2 million dollars in today's dollars. She is fully satisfied with meeting her definition of lower-order needs at the basic and safety levels. Social needs are met through her connections with and activities at the university. Natalie is a member of a prestigious social club. She perceives herself as a welcomed colleague in all regards. Others offer reinforcement through association, friendship, and nominations for awards. Also, she does volunteer work with veterans who aspire to be entrepreneurs. Understandably, she feels good about herself and her station in life.

She is a likely candidate to reach self-actualization and perhaps even self-transcendence. Natalie has realized her definition of happiness.

Although Dr. T. may have ascended within Maslow's hierarchy, there is no guarantee that she will be so positioned for any period of time. Suppose the contract at the university enables staff and faculty reduction if programs are cut. She may be forced to seek alternative employment. If financial security is brought into question, club membership might be of nominal importance. Things change, sometimes abruptly. What was once a satisfying connection with virtually all facets of life could suddenly shift to unexpected turbulence. Negative impact with a job or health or relationships, in addition to other life events, can disrupt an otherwise smooth journey.

People are motivated on a variety of levels and for different reasons. Choices must be made, or a decision is made by default. Satisfaction of needs in an industrialized nation leans more toward satisfying wants. Are the wants of consumable products likely to outweigh the want of accumulating wealth?

The discussion of Maslow's hierarchy illustrates that choices are made throughout our lifetime that reflect our developed characteristics leading toward or away from self-actualization.[81] Some choose more conservative approaches to finding satisfaction within the needs/want continuum and thus are able to please themselves and enhance wealth building.

Vignette: Happiness Merged with Millions

Mr. Charles is a twice-divorced sixty-six-year-old who is worth $8 million. His score of twenty-nine out of thirty-five on the subjective well-being scale suggests that he is happy with his life. (More about this scale in the next chapter.) After his father was fired from a sales job at age fifty, Mr.

Charles was inspired to become entrepreneurial and to work for himself by buying a radio station. Highly leveraged, he invested $20,000 and borrowed nearly $600,000. He was nervous for the next three years, as the numbers didn't work, contributing to the demise of his first marriage. Nevertheless, he understood that cash flow is the key to success. Drawing on a statistics course from college, he was able to develop a clear picture about the market the radio station reached, or more importantly, the market it could reach. Eventually, he was able to make the station profitable.

There was no need for a prenuptial agreement with his first marriage, as he had no money! For his second marriage, even with a prenuptial, the divorce was still tied up for five years with legal squabbles. Finally, his ex-wife settled because she ran out of money to continue the fight. He averred: "My net worth was protected by a miracle."

The two marriages produced four children. He delights in having them vacation at his lakeside cottage. While he helped his children to graduate from college debt free, he is not inclined to provide extraordinary gifts for them. Instead, he notes they look to him for encouragement, no matter their career choices. One of his sons joined him in buying a weekly newspaper, which they subsequently sold at a profit.

Mr. Charles says he will never retire, but by age sixty, he felt more inclined to acquire more liquid assets. He is diversified with 28 percent bonds, 28 percent stocks, 28 percent small businesses, and the rest in cash and his cottage. Interestingly, he fired his stock broker/manager, who charged a 1 percent fee, even in underperforming markets. Now he relies on low-cost index funds that he selects himself.

So where does Mr. Charles go from here? Currently his income is $250,000 and he still saves $45,000 annually. As he reflects on his life, he hopes to give more to charity. He grew up with the lessons of Matthew 25 and knows that he is obliged to help the dispossessed of society. In his summary: "I want my money to grow, so I can give away a lot of it." He considers himself a self-actualized person.

WE ARE THE CUSTODIANS

When all is considered, we don't own much, no matter how much wealth we may have accumulated. We don't *own* our health; we are the caretakers of it. We have God-given freewill, thus some choose to abuse themselves with addictive substances or practices (including workaholics) and others prioritize a healthy lifestyle. Of course, there is no escape from death, but perhaps awareness of the leading causes provides a cautionary warning. According to the National Center for Health Statistics, the most frequent causes of death are those shown in Table 4-2.[82] Country singer Hank Williams's words will resonate forever: "I'll never get out of this life alive."

There will always be challenges affecting our decision-making and the resulting consequences.

Table 4-2
Causes of Death in 2014

Cause	Number
Heart disease	614,348
Cancer	591,699
Chronic lower respiratory diseases	147,101
Accidents (unintentional injuries)	136,053
Stroke (cerebrovascular diseases)	133,103
Alzheimer's disease	93,541
Diabetes	76,488
Influenza and pneumonia	55,227
Nephritis, nephrotic syndrome, and nephrosis	48,146
Intentional self-harm (suicide)	42,773

Source: National Center for Health Statistics

Getting Personal

Dear Drs. WDD and RVN,

By today's fitness standards, I am considered obese. However, at 6' 1" I wear my 242 pounds well. I am financially successful with multiple new car dealerships.

I have a ten-hour workday six days a week. If I shorten my workweek, I feel that I will risk having lower profitability. Of course, the upside would be more time for R&R and effort toward physical fitness.

My question is: How do I balance my work and personal life?

Big Guy

Dear Big Guy,

Poverty of time is always a challenge. After all, time is a nonrenewable resource.

You don't mention your eating habits or stress level. Since you have multiple car dealerships, we would hope that your managers would be trusted to run each. If not, perhaps you need to review your organizational structure along with your corporate policies. Of course, it is easier to manage with clear goals and objectives.

In terms of balance between work and personal time, personality comes into the picture. Further, your value system will dictate your choices. Health should be at the top of your concerns. Without good health, what can you accomplish over an extended period of time?

Proper diet and moderate exercise are the usual recommendations. Choose the right management people to run your dealerships, and place trust in your decisions to let them do their job. Have alternate plans drafted to handle inevitable business issues. Delegate, and be sure that managers given responsibility have the matching authority to act.

WHAT DO WE REALLY OWN?

We don't *own* our children. We have custody of them, and most people try to do the very best they can to instill optimal values as their children grow to mature adults.

Of course, there is a challenge to successfully impart first-class values and provide desired financial support given all of the contemporary interference factors. And indeed, the financial responsibility is significant.

A report from the U.S. Department of Agriculture reveals the cost of raising a child[83] from birth through age 17, is now $233,610. This is based on a two-child, middle income, married-couple family. A breakdown of the costs follows: 29 percent for housing; 18 percent for food; 16 percent for child care and education; 15 percent for transportation; 9 percent for health care; 7 percent for miscellaneous; and 6 percent for clothing.

Getting Personal

Dear Drs. WDD and RVN,

My husband and I have three beautiful children ages 4, 7, and 9. We are planning oriented and as we look to the future we try to calculate, as best we can, how to provide for our children through their college years and then for our own retirement. Is there a general framework as an overview for long-range family financial planning?

Priscilla Planner

Dear Priscilla,

Most likely, the best approach would be to meet with a competent and trusted professional financial planner. There is much published data on costs of raising a child and the cost of a college education. So there is no shortage of information on current and forecasted costs that pertain to your family.

Overall, we are glad to hear that you are planners and as such you should do some homework to gather preliminary data and information prior to meeting with a professional financial planner. At a minimum, you should prepare a current balance sheet, a budget, and pro forma financial statements for future expectations.

Just remember that a plan set to writing should be a fluid and not a static document.

We don't *own* our money in the long term. Sure, we have the right to buy all sorts of consumable products, boats, cars, expensive clothing, and the like—or we can choose to invest in stocks, bonds, commodities, real estate, or some other asset mix. But eventually some other person or entity will take possession of it.

Our freewill is empowerment to make decisions. Is a healthy lifestyle practiced? Do we create a homegrown culture of superfluous stuff for ourselves and/or for our children? Or do we create a nurturing environment?

Do we decide to live large or live below our means in order to save/invest for the future?

Never forget to clearly differentiate between real needs and frivolous wants. After all, we are custodians. What seeds are we planting for the next generation?

Personal attributes are discussed in chapter 5 to help you understand what may be done to find true prosperity. Further, we examine what it takes to be happy. Of course, being happy *and* rich is a bonus.

Happiness

IS HAPPINESS EVEN NECESSARY?

A pundit[84] posed the question: Why is being happy superior to not being happy? Shouldn't both be thought of as psychiatric disorders? While it is interesting to pose such questions, the empirical evidence is in favor of seeking happiness, and the benefits of being happy are overwhelming.

Psychologists who study happiness find that "happy people participate more in community organizations, are more liked by others, are less likely to get divorced, tend to live slightly longer, perform better at work, and even earn higher incomes. Thus, high levels of SWB [subjective well-being] might be beneficial for a society, and no evidence indicates they would be harmful."[85] So, "[w]ho is happy? Knowing a person's age, sex, race, and income (assuming the person has enough to afford life's necessities) hardly give a clue. Better clues come from knowing a person's traits, whether the person enjoys a supportive network of close relationships, whether the person's culture offers positive interpretations for most daily events, whether the person is engaged by work and leisure, and whether the person has a faith that entails social support, purpose, and hope."[86]

A MEDICAL VIEW

A practicing psychiatrist and professor emeritus at the Albert Einstein College of Medicine with over forty-five years of experience, T. Byram Karasu concludes that true happiness is found in God, and only by striving to be godly will we achieve a meaningful existence. Doctor Karasu reminds us that there are many popular books that examine happiness and the meaning of life. However, he needs just one reference to make his case: the Holy Bible. He dismisses the rest, by affirming that "the works of secular gurus demonstrate again and again that making the mind of man its own center generates only personal confusion, unhappiness, and communal disorders...Only by being godly can you be strong and successful, find joy and happiness, and live an extraordinarily meaningful existence while leading an ordinary life." [87]

Doctor Karasu's statements might appear a bit strong, until one considers survey research evidence about physicians and their patients. A US study of 1,044 (non-psychiatrist) physicians found that 90 percent have a religious affiliation, 77 percent believe in God, and 60 percent believe in an afterlife. The same study included a subset of 100 psychiatrists. Their percentages were somewhat lower on all three measures: 83 percent of psychiatrists have a religious affiliation, 65 percent believe in God, and 42 percent believe in an afterlife. The authors concluded that psychiatrists and other physicians were equally likely to say that their religious beliefs influence their practice of medicine. Thus they should work to see that these differences "do not unduly compromise patients' opportunities to receive appropriate spiritual or psychiatric care." [88] In another paper using the same data, more than three-quarters of all physicians "often or always" feel that "religion/spirituality helps patients to cope with and endure illness and suffering." [89] Consistent with this finding, a Canadian study of 88 clinically depressed inpatients found that those who regularly attend church and pray recover more quickly (and have a higher satisfaction with life) than their nonreligious counterparts. [90]

DECLARATION OF INDEPENDENCE

On July 4, 1776, the Second Continental Congress adopted the Declaration of Independence, capturing the sentiments of our founding fathers and setting the stage for what was to become the greatest country on earth. In part, this document declares, "We hold these Truths to be self-evident, that all Men are created equal, that they are endowed by their Creator with certain unalienable Rights, that among these are Life, Liberty, and the Pursuit of Happiness." No doubt these words were inspired by Aristotle's work on ethics written in 350 BC: "Happiness, then, is something final and self-sufficient, and is the end of action."[91] It is health, wealth, friendship, knowledge, and virtue—all good things—that lead to happiness, according to Aristotle. Thus our level of happiness defines our whole human life.

The evidence shows that our founding fathers understood the timelessness of human nature. They knew it was imperative to ensure an environment in which one would be free to pursue happiness. They knew that this kind of environment would be critical in creating opportunities for society and individuals. In our view, they were right. Collectively, let us work to ensure the same for future generations.

NEED FOR INSPIRATION

Twentieth-century American statesman Dean Alfange's (1899–1989) social commentary about not wanting to be a common man has been cited in numerous publications and speeches. Along with various alterations, it has been used to inspire entrepreneurs, and even dentists. Some versions mention God. It has even been mistakenly attributed to one of America's founding fathers, Thomas Paine. It first appeared in 1951 in *This Week* magazine. His wisdom is extolled in the following creed:

I do not choose to be a common man. It is my right to be uncommon – if I can. I seek opportunity – not security. I do not wish to be a kept citizen, humbled and dulled by having the state look after me.

I want to take the calculated risk; to dream and to build, to fail and to succeed. I refuse to barter incentive for a dole. I prefer the challenges of life to the guaranteed existence; the thrill of fulfillment to the stale calm of utopia.

I will not trade freedom for beneficence or my dignity for a handout. I will never cower before any master nor bend to any threat. It is my heritage to stand erect, proud and unafraid; to think and act for myself, enjoy the benefit of my creations and to face the world boldly and say, this I have done.

All this is what it means to be an American.[92]

MEASURING HAPPINESS

The satisfaction with life scale (SWLS) is a widely used, reliable, and valid measure in the public domain that measures subjective well-being (SWB).[93] SWB is a term synonymous with happiness. On a seven-point scale,[94] where higher values indicate greater agreement, individuals provide responses to five statements:

- In most ways my life is close to my ideal.

- The conditions of my life are excellent.

- I am satisfied with my life.

- So far I have gotten the important things I want in life.

- If I could live my life over, I would change almost nothing.

Summing the one- to seven-point scores across the five items produces a scale that ranges from five to thirty-five. Users of this scale[95] typically interpret score results as follows: twenty-one or more points indicates that one is satisfied with life, twenty points is neutral, and nineteen or fewer points indicates that one is dissatisfied with life.

Of course, this measure, while reliable and valid, only addresses life *so far*. It does not address the future.

During a pretest of our questionnaire, a Roman Catholic priest urged the inclusion of a measure regarding future expectations. He suggested:

- Quite often I feel anxious when I think about the future.

Considering the source, it is easy to see the appeal of this statement, as it is rooted in the power of God. For example, Alcoholics Anonymous is centered on the theme "let go and let God." This organization recognizes that only a higher power can direct us in a battle over addiction.

Those who are not anxious have a serenity found among true believers in God. Again, this is irrespective of material wealth. It is hard to argue with the virtue of not being anxious.

Response to the new statement about anxiety is highly correlated with the measure of subjective well-being.[96] Although the relationship is not perfect, the inverse direction of the relationship is consistent with the SWB scale. Thus it is possible to rate low in current subjective well-being but be comfortable about the future and free of anxiety. One can imagine a person who is currently experiencing hard times but is an optimist. Likewise, those ranking high on current happiness might be anxious about the future and wrestling with their inner selves. This might describe a person who knew it couldn't last and has no real direction in life.

Let us expand on these combinations by highlighting some specific examples. Table 5-1 allows us to systematically examine four scenarios based on current levels of satisfaction and how anxious one is about the future. Quadrant A: True Riches, includes two examples: one from an up-and-comer and the other from a millionaire. Both show that "true riches" go beyond mere money. Quadrant D: Hedonist, is illustrated by a physician. The remaining two quadrants—B: Patience of Job and C: Disaster—are illustrated with examples of millionaires. Generalizations cannot be made with these limited examples, of course, but they do serve to humanize the data.

Table 5-1
Future Anxiety and Current Satisfaction

	Current Satisfaction	
	Low SWB Score between 5 and 19:	High SWB Score between 21 and 35:
Future Anxiety	Dissatisfied	Satisfied
Not anxious about the future	B: Patience of Job	A: True Riches
Anxious about the future	C: Disaster	D: Hedonist

A: TRUE RICHES—MR. YOUNG

Mr. Young is a forty-one-year-old corporate executive. He earns more than $500,000 annually and has built a net worth in excess of $2.5 million. Married once and never divorced, he and his wife are raising two children under twelve years of age. He's in great physical shape. His house has a market value of $1.3 million. It appears he has led a charmed life, until you appreciate his personal struggle:

> I am recovering from alcoholism. Alcoholism was caused by my drive to succeed and perfectionism. My life-changing event was the realization that no matter the degree of material and professional success, happiness and self-esteem are derived from the soul. I am fortunate to be provided opportunities that enabled me to achieve material and professional success, but the cost was my personal happiness.

Mr. Young has a true sense of gratitude that he was able to overcome his addiction and reach a prosperous and balanced life. His SWB score is twenty-eight. He indicates that he is not anxious about the future. He also reports that God is central to his life.

A: TRUE RICHES—DR. DENISE

Dr. Denise is a radiologist. Just thirty-eight years old, she and her physician husband earn nearly $500,000 annually. Their net worth is less than $600,000. How can their earning power be so good, and yet they have a low net worth? They are givers, she especially.

For business purposes, she and her husband keep their finances separate. Her school debt has been paid off; she is an up-and-comer. She has a flexible work schedule that allows her to spend time with her young son and to help others in need. She insists that spending time with loved ones is important, as life is short. Where did she develop this orientation?

> I was an "army brat," often moving from base to base. My parents are now divorced, but I had a mentor in college. He recognized my ability in the sciences and encouraged me to aim high. Instead of being "just a teacher," he told me I could be a physician! I also have a number of Christian preachers in my family. At a very young age, I was told "we can't store up treasures on earth." Combined, my earning ability—especially with a fee-based, time-flexible practice—and my firm beliefs, I am obligated to help others. For example, I helped set up a clinic to bring ultrasound services to poor pregnant women. My goal is to inspire my son to embrace the same values.

Dr. Denise is not only a practicing Christian, but she also affirms that God is central to her life. Her SWB score is twenty-six, and she is not anxious about the future.

B: PATIENCE OF JOB—MR. BURDEN

The Old Testament book of Job was written between the seventh and fifth centuries BC. Job was a prosperous man who lost all of his property and suffered the deaths of his children. Yet he did not blame God; his faith sustained him.

One of the most difficult stories of hardship also has a redeeming quality. Mr. Burden faced extreme hardships but never lost his faith.

Mr. Burden is a fifty-six-year-old college-educated married man with a net worth in excess of $3 million. He related the following story:

> My biggest life-changing event was when my oldest son came home on Christmas day two and a half years ago with his arms and neck covered with tattoos. I have not seen him since and never want to see him again. He was everything to me. I had prostate cancer, my wife is a b***h, and my business has been in very bad shape for the past three years. I have worked seventy-five to eighty-five hours a week, seven days a week for the past three years without pay, and with only about four days off. I have lost well over half my net worth.

What is the redeeming quality? He scored a six on the subjective well-being scale, placing him very low on current life satisfaction. However, Mr. Burden is also quick to point out that he is not anxious about the future. He strongly believes in a spiritual life after physical death. Although he only rates himself as a three on his commitment to his Protestant religion (on a ten-point scale), he affirms that God is central to his life. Truly, with God, you are never alone—Mr. Burden has unwavering faith that all is for a reason and that eventually all will be satisfactorily resolved.

C: DISASTER—DR. PAIN

Dr. Pain is a fifty-five-year-old dentist. Despite a $2 million net worth and a $400,000 annual salary, he is angry. He is divorced, has under-employed adult children, and is in ill health.

> My twenty-fifth anniversary present from my wife was leaving me for my alcoholic neighbor. I spent thirty years sleeping with

the enemy. I have three great children, but their mother is the Devil…so who knows how "great" they really are. I guess I want to spend my last dollar as I take my last breath.

Dr. Pain scores a thirteen on the subjective well-being measure, and he strongly agrees that he is anxious about the future. He does not believe in an afterlife; God is not central to his life. He has nothing to look forward to, wanting "to spend my last dollar as I take my last breath."

C: DISASTER—FRUSTRATED AND CONFUSED

Consider a recent e-mail from a frustrated and confused multimillionaire who is seemingly satisfied with life in a secular sense, and even that presents huge problems. You will note that this individual has some serious issues to resolve.

Getting Personal

Dear Drs. WDD and RVN,

I have a few issues that I would like for you to comment on.

I am forty-four years old. In 2000, I started a transportation company by borrowing money from everyone I knew. Thank God, things worked out for the best. I make a fairly large salary, have a net worth of over $3M, and don't have a penny in my bank account.

I borrowed money up to my eyeballs in 2000 to start the business. For the first few months, I was having a very difficult time paying my mortgage. My salary was very low back then. After about a year, my investments appreciated fairly rapidly (they doubled within the first two years). I was able to pay everyone back and refinance for a much lower interest rate.

Now, I'm sure you've heard this story before: with some of my newfound equity, I went and bought a high-end BMW. Fortunately, once again, my investments appreciated, and I was able to pay off my car in full.

In the meantime, I met and fell in love with a beautiful girl, who I can't find the guts to say no to. Before her, I never bought $2,000 suits; I never had $700 shoes. She convinced me that wearing expensive clothing would make me more successful. In addition, she would be much happier with $500 jeans, $5,000 dresses, and $3,500 handbags.

Once again, I find myself back where I started. I may not have been the greatest at saving money, but even with such a low salary back then, I was able to put aside a few dollars. After I met my wife, I now have a $600,000 apartment. She drives a Porsche, and I drive a $100,000 Mercedes. You can imagine my monthly expenses and cost of living. Furthermore, she forced me to put about $150,000 worth of renovations into our new apartment. I had to borrow this money; I am way overleveraged.

I know I'm in a tough situation, and I'm making it sound like I'm not willing to help or work with myself. But it is a tough situation. My wife takes after her mother who is a spendaholic and exhausts any credit card within minutes of possession.

Please reply. I would like to hear your thoughts.

Regards,
Frustrated and Confused

In a follow-up interview with "Frustrated and Confused," despite a net worth of over $3 million (none of which was from an inheritance), he scored very low (a seven) on the subjective well-being scale. This suggests that his substantial investments and entrepreneurial zeal produce a meager cash flow that is not capable of keeping up with his new lifestyle. Interestingly, he feels that a $300 million net worth—one hundred times his current level—would give him a feeling of being rich enough in material wealth. But he assigns a low probability that he will ever achieve this goal.

In many ways, "Frustrated and Confused" knows the source of his temporary problem. He has to get spending under control. It is clear that he has a tremendous ability to increase his net worth were it not for the woman he can't say no to.

Some other important clues about his problem: God is not part of his life. He does not give of himself in a larger sense, neither by volunteering his time nor by giving his riches to others. He admits that he is anxious about the future.

D: HEDONIST—DR. MARTIN

Dr. Martin is a hedonist who is anxious about the future. He scores a twenty-nine on the satisfaction index and has a household net worth of nearly $2 million, easily placing him in the "satisfied millionaire" category. He seems to lead an active life with skiing, hiking, and volunteer work. Further, he claims to be a practicing Catholic. In fact, his parents hoped he would attend the seminary. While he joins his two preteen children—both of whom attend a parochial school—along with his physician wife at church services, there is something missing in his life.

Most millionaire physicians insist that God is central to their life and that there is an afterlife, but not Dr. Martin, who is anxious about the future. This contrast is summarized in Table 5-2.

Table 5-2

Contrast Dr. Martin with a Sample of Millionaire Physicians

Characteristic	Millionaire Physicians n=57	Dr. Martin
Subjective Well-Being Score	27.1	29.0
I am anxious about the future.	70.2% disagree	agree
God is central to my life.	52.6% agree	disagree
There is a spiritual life after physical death.	56.1% agree	disagree
Prayer's only benefit is psychological.	65.0% disagree	agree
I have a religious affiliation.	86% yes	yes

Vignette: Harmony of Faith

Frank W., an unemployed construction engineer, was very active in his church and volunteered to teach adult education classes. He believed that his Christian service had earned him some special merit with the Almighty. He believed that if he prayed hard enough then what he needed would be provided—and he needed a job, especially since his resources were dwindling, as was his self-esteem.

He forgot the adage that suggests we pray as if all is in the hands of God but work as if all is in our hands. After many hours of praying, beseeching others to pray for him, and attending extra services, he watched as weeks went by with no results. All of this was to no avail. He was angry and frustrated. What was Frank doing wrong? Just praying isn't enough to generate a job offer. Odds are quite slim that prayerful action will do much without worldly proactive action.

Getting Personal

Dear Drs. WDD and RVN,

Oh yeah, life is good—for now. I have what I want and I want what I have. As a married twenty-six-year-old with two kids, I am happy and having a good life. My wife and I have all the toys—motor home, boat, ATVs, and a beachfront condo. I'm a Wall Street guy, and all is well, especially at bonus time. I earn about $480,000 a year. My net worth is approaching $2 million.

I'm maxing out my retirement plan and other tax-deferred plans in addition to market investments.

On occasion I wonder: Will this go on forever? And what if it doesn't? How do I mentally prepare for the possibility of both shoes dropping?

Ira Living Large

Dear Ira,

Great to hear you are enjoying the good life and that all of you are healthy and happy.

It is always wise to not get overly confident that good things will last forever. Recall the parable of the rich fool.[97] On the spiritual side of the good life, our research reveals that the majority of satisfied millionaires state that God is central in their lives. It seems a valuable connection!

On the pragmatic side, be sure to continue accruing wealth and be cautious about excessive enjoyment.

The fact that you stop and ask the question about permanence demonstrates that you are a realist.

Carry on!

THE BIGGER PICTURE

These anecdotes help us to get an understanding of the issues. Next, we present a summary of our study findings of selected characteristics of dissatisfied and satisfied millionaires and dissatisfied and satisfied up-and-comers to give a broader perspective. Tables 5-3 and 5-4 provide details.

Table 5-3
Selected Characteristics of Dissatisfied and Satisfied
Millionaires

| Selected Characteristic | Millionaires | | | |
	Dissatisfied n=84	Satisfied n=699	t	P(t)
Behavioral or Life Choices				
Percent of income given to charity	4.02	5.61	-3.39	0.001
Average hours volunteered yearly	33.60	101.61	-5.51	0.000
Percent who enjoy volunteering	16.67	35.19	-4.14	0.000
Percent registered as Republican	44.05	55.36	-1.97	0.049
Percent registered as Democrat	23.81	20.46	0.71	0.475
Percent married and never divorced	66.67	77.68	-2.25	0.024
Percent separated or divorced	11.90	3.72	2.26	0.026
Percent belonging to a religion	91.67	90.84	0.25	0.804
Percent who pray	15.48	24.75	-2.16	0.033
Psychological				
Percent agreeing that…				
God is central to their lives	41.67	55.22	-2.36	0.019
They are anxious about the future	59.52	29.47	5.65	0.000
They are at peace with their soul	41.67	89.13	-8.57	0.000
Demographic				
Average age	55.65	54.30	1.34	0.181
Percent men	84.52	79.40	1.11	0.268
Percent white	96.43	93.56	1.28	0.203
Average years of education	17.38	17.27	0.49	0.623

Table 5-4
Selected Characteristics of Dissatisfied and Satisfied
"up-and-comers"

| Selected Characteristic | "up-and-comers" | | | |
	Dissatisfied n=120	Satisfied n=408	t	P(t)
Behavioral or Life Choices				
Percent of income given to charity	3.92	4.59	-1.55	0.121
Average hours volunteered yearly	50.79	71.72	-1.41	0.161
Percent who enjoy volunteering	28.33	41.18	-2.56	0.011
Percent registered as Republican	38.33	49.02	-2.07	0.039
Percent registered as Democrat	35.83	25.74	2.17	0.030
Percent married and never divorced	61.67	69.36	-1.58	0.114
Percent separated or divorced	12.50	7.84	1.41	0.162
Percent belonging to a religion	95.00	92.65	0.99	0.324
Percent who pray	23.33	34.31	-2.28	0.023
Psychological				
Percent agreeing that…				
God is central to their lives	56.67	68.14	-2.33	0.020
They are anxious about the future	64.17	36.03	5.63	0.000
They are at peace with their soul	55.00	87.75	-6.76	0.000
Demographic				
Average age	53.20	51.16	2.33	0.021
Percent men	65.83	66.42	-0.12	0.905
Percent white	89.17	92.16	-0.95	0.343
Average years of education	16.58	16.90	-1.45	0.147

Rather than offering an opinion based on feelings, we can have a specified level of confidence in our statements, if we turn to the field of inferential statistics. When we have two mutually exclusive and independent groups, as we have in the tables, a t-test of differences is appropriate. The last columns in Table 5-3 and Table 5-4 show the probability of the difference between the groups occurring by chance. For example, the first entry in Table 5-3 shows a value of .001. This indicates that the chance that 4.02 and 5.61 are equal, based on these samples, is one in a thousand, which is unlikely. They could be equal, but 999 times out of 1000, we would conclude that they differ, based on similar samples. For our interpretation, any probability less than 5 percent (.05) suggests a meaningful difference between the groups.

Three broad categories are considered: behavioral or life choices, psychological, and demographic characteristics. The results show that there are no substantial differences between dissatisfied and satisfied millionaires based solely on demographic characteristics. Each group can be described as middle-aged college-educated white men. We determined this based on the large probabilities shown in the last column.

To be clear, a wide range of ages, both genders, and other races were included in the samples. However, their numbers were too sparse to allow for meaningful interpretations. There are, however, meaningful differences when we examine the other characteristics.

Satisfied millionaires donate more time and money to charity when compared to dissatisfied millionaires. They are also more likely to be registered as Republicans and married and never divorced. Both groups claim to belong to a religion, but satisfied millionaires are more likely to pray. Consistent with prayer, we find that satisfied millionaires are more likely to say that God is central to their lives, that they are not anxious about the future, and that they are at peace with their souls.

In a similar manner, we can examine dissatisfied and satisfied up-and-comers, groups that have a net worth of at least $100,000 but under $1,000,000, as shown in Table 5-4. Here, of the sixteen characteristics measured, eight show the groups could be similar, and eight show a statistical difference.

The satisfied up-and-comers are slightly younger than those who are dissatisfied. Both groups can be described as college-educated white men. The satisfied group enjoys volunteering and is more likely to be registered as Republicans.

When it comes to prayer and psychological characteristics, the satisfied up-and-comer shows a similar pattern to the satisfied millionaire. The satisfied group is more prayerful, more likely to indicate that God is central to their lives, less anxious about the future, and is at peace with their souls.

WHERE DO YOU STAND?

The subjective well-being test is provided in Table 5-5 for your self-assessment. Indicate your level of agreement to the five statements shown, and calculate your score that will range from a low of five to a high of thirty-five.

If the SWB score ranges from five to nineteen, one would be classified as dissatisfied. A score of twenty is neutral. A score that ranges from twenty-one to thirty-five indicates one is satisfied.

Table 5-5
Calculating Subjective Well-Being (SWB)

Statement	Level of Agreement						
	Strongly Disagree	Disagree	Slightly Disagree	Neither Agree nor Disagree	Slightly Agree	Agree	Strongly Agree
In most ways my life is close to my ideal.	1	2	3	4	5	6	7
The conditions of my life are excellent.	1	2	3	4	5	6	7
I am satisfied with my life.	1	2	3	4	5	6	7
So far I have gotten the important things I want in life.	1	2	3	4	5	6	7
If I could live my life over, I would change almost nothing.	1	2	3	4	5	6	7

The vignette that follows tells the story of a "searcher" who eventually, through behavior modification, found life satisfaction. Indeed, true prosperity.

Vignette: Robert W.—A Purpose Greater than Himself

Robert is worth $4.9 million, including his primary residence. This is really amazing, considering he is now on his third marriage. The first marriage ended amicably after twenty years, producing a son and a daughter. Robert is very close to them, with his daughter working in his business. The second marriage was a "refinement" but lasted just ten years. With this experience, he developed a list of twenty characteristics his next spouse must have. Now in his fifth year with number three, he scores thirty-four out of thirty-five on the happiness scale (SWB). For the record, though, number three also contributed a little more than half of his current net worth.

When Robert graduated from college, he married his high school sweetheart and got a job just to pay the bills. Now at fifty-five, he has found a lucrative niche as a business consultant, book publisher, and landlord collecting rents. His pretax income is nearly $200,000. He readily admits that he is not smart, just blessed. He thanks God for his health and plans to work forever, as he loves what he does.

He also attributes his success to his well-honed sales skills. He wanted more than a job; he wanted to prove he could be an achiever. However, he also knows that personal services, where he is the salesman *and* the one who delivers, are naturally limited by the number of hours in the day. The better model for him included rents and selling books. He is delighted that his daughter will succeed him in the publishing business. As he remarked, she has put her soul into it. No doubt this contributes to his life satisfaction.

Robert has enough money. He says he wants to continue working so he can give more to charity. Through his businesses, he is able to use money for a greater purpose.

A PHILOSOPHY TO CONSIDER

"What I have discovered is that happiness is entirely up to me. Others in my life can add to or diminish my happiness somewhat. But the key to knowing and living happiness is to accept that happiness is my choice alone. And I choose it every time. Lucky me!"

—EDITH M. DONOHUE, PhD

Chapter 6 provides specific proactive steps that may be taken on the pathway to becoming richer than a millionaire.

THINGS YOU CAN DO TO
REACH TRUE PROSPERITY

We all make choices. Even when we don't choose, a choice is made by default. Individuals frequently ensure poor decision making by failing to obtain even the most basic information necessary to make intelligent choices.

We must be proactive, explore facts, and then make well-informed decisions. This chapter highlights pathway-to-prosperity options along with suggested actions to take.

PROFILE YOURSELF

In chapter 5, you were given the opportunity to calculate your personal SWB score. If you did not do this, do so now. This score provides some guidance.

WHAT'S IN YOUR VALUE SYSTEM?

Revisit chapter 3 for a listing of values. Add more if you don't find what you prioritize as valued in your life. The important thing is to know what your motivating hot buttons are.

FORGET THE JONESES

A recent study examined the impact of lottery winners' spending behaviors on their neighbors' spending behaviors. Surprisingly, the authors found that a 1 percent increase in the lottery prize causes a .04 percent increase in subsequent bankruptcies among the winners' close neighbors. The size of the lottery prize increased the amount of visible assets, such as houses, automobiles, etc., that were listed by the bankrupt neighbors. However, the invisible assets, such as cash and other financial assets, were not affected by the size of the lottery winnings. [98] The bottom line is that trying to keep up with the Joneses will lead to financial distress.

PRACTICE THE GOLDEN RULE

In our survey, respondents noted whether they agreed with the following statement: I live by the Golden Rule, loving my neighbor as myself. The vast majority—80 percent of the millionaires and 84 percent of the up-and-comers—claim to live by the Golden Rule.

Vignette: The Grandviews and the Golden Rule

Mr. and Mrs. Grandview are serial entrepreneurs. She is a forty-nine-year-old college graduate who grew up in a household where money was a routine part of the conversation. Her mother owned a collection agency, and her father worked for a finance company and later was a VP at a bank. In contrast, her thirty-seven-year-old husband is a college dropout, was brought up on a farm, and had parents who instilled in him the difference between price and value. The emphasis was always on being a value-oriented buyer of goods and services. Both were the only children of their parents. Neither received a monetary inheritance. Yet they are now multimillionaires.

After Mrs. Grandview finished college, she took a job as a secretary and then became a paralegal in corporate law. At the same time, she began selling cosmetics on a part-time basis. This led her into the top 3 percent of all producers while managing fifty people in whose commissions she shared. She became convinced that self-employment would be her future path. Mr. Grandview has always been self-employed. This made their views compatible.

While the Grandviews have no children of their own, they participated in the Big Sister program, nurturing a young woman. They encouraged her to graduate from high school, get an apartment, and become gainfully employed. They proudly say that they helped her become self-sufficient by instilling their values and giving her life skills that her biological parents were unwilling to do.

The Grandviews embrace the Earl Nightingale admonition about cause and effect. The often-cited anecdote of the man telling the wood burning stove to "give me heat and then I will give you wood" sums it up. They know that giving must precede getting. This was certainly reflected in their work with the Big Sister program. It also is reflected in their restaurant business.

For the past five years, the Grandviews have owned two—and shortly will own three—fast-food franchises. They own the real estate and enjoy the good name of the restaurants. They delight in the idea that they can nurture young people in this service industry. Industrywide, employee turnover approaches 200 percent annually. Their restaurants average 44 percent.

The Grandviews earn $400,000 annually, largely from the restaurants and a warehouse and landscape business they own. They own a lakeside cottage. They enjoy assets that appreciate in value. So far, so good. However, they are concerned about the future.

This couple hopes to retire one day and live off the cash flow from their existing businesses. A real impediment they lament is that the work ethic of the 1950s is vanishing. They know that a work ethic is important, and they hope to instill this essential value into all of their employees.

Millionaires and up-and-comers alike are more satisfied with life when they practice the Golden Rule, as shown in Figure 6-1.

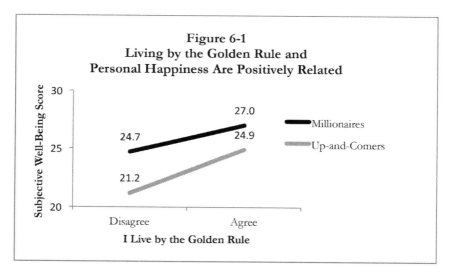

Figure 6-1
Living by the Golden Rule and
Personal Happiness Are Positively Related

Our survey results show that the increase in the SWB scores for both groups are statistically significant.[99]

Of course, there are many points of view related to principles for behavior. One such opinion follows.

Getting Personal

Dear Drs. WDD and RVN,

I belong to no formal religious group or church, but I consider myself a believer and feel connected at a spiritual level. I donate about 4 percent of my earnings to various charities.

The Golden Rule is something that I am not so sure about since it presumes that others would agree with your own interpretation of fairness and expectation. Would you give insider-trader information that you accidentally discovered to a friend because you would expect that friend to do the same for you? Illegal, yes, but it does follow the Golden Rule principle, does it not?

I feel pleased with all in my life; am I missing something?

Doubting Thomas

Dear Thomas,

As with most brief rules of behavior, each one is itself subject to interpretation. A few follow: the Golden Rule is that there are no golden rules (George Bernard Shaw); know the rules well, so you can break them effectively (Dalai Lama XIV); hell, there are no rules here—we're trying to accomplish something (Thomas A. Edison).[100]

In all seriousness, though, the Golden Rule that we reference in our study focuses on a genuine charity toward others. Practicing that will likely increase your personal happiness.

KEEP YOUR DEBT UNDER CONTROL

So, who owes? According to the Federal Reserve, three quarters of all households carry some debt. The average mortgage debt is $182,421 for households that still carry a mortgage. The highest mortgage debt is held by those between the ages of 45 and 54. The highest student loan debt is held by those under 35 years of age. The average balance for student loans is $50,626. The highest debt for auto loans is held by those 35 to 54 years of age. The average amount owed for auto loans is $29,539. For those with credit card debt the average load is $16,883. Credit card debt is highest for those 45 to 54 years of age.[101]

Why do people go into debt? Well, the short answer is that at a very basic level we want to improve our standard of living. Perhaps we invest in ourselves with ongoing education. However, many times we just want more stuff. Unless we're born into wealth or have success with winning a large sum of money in a lottery, we do need some amount of debt to live the dream. Debt has upsides and, of course, downsides. Investing requires careful vetting of all "opportunities." The equation of reward and risk must always be considered.

Getting Personal

Dear Drs. WDD and RVN,

What's luck got to do with it? Maybe a lot. The cloud of doom seems to follow me.

I've invested in the stock market and lost; I bought real estate that I can't sell because, two years after the purchase, it was designated a wetland; I loaned money to a friend to start a "can't lose" business, and it did. What the heck! I went into debt with all of this.

So how do I pick up the pieces, regroup, and change my luck? I have a six-figure income, and I feel like I'm bleeding money from a thousand cuts.

Please help!

Unlucky Eddy

Dear Eddy,

Indeed, the cloud of doom. Who knows about luck? Good, bad, or indifferent, it happens.

Calculated risk is key. Unfortunately, no infallible crystal ball exists. Many people have lost money in the stock market, and yet many people have made money too. Obviously, the market can be a wild roller coaster ride given uncertain economic conditions. Real estate has, in general, been an asset that appreciates in value over time. But, as you point out, unforeseen things happen. A failed business always causes collateral damage. Not sure to what extent you went into debt for your investments? Hopefully, it is not so extreme that it prevents recovery.

Careful research is a prudent course of action. In order to regroup, you need to assess where you stand financially after your run of bad luck. Prepare your current balance sheet. Assuming you have liquid assets (cash), where will you invest? Always be on guard when you hear the words "can't lose." Do you use a competent financial advisor? Did you purchase your real estate through a licensed agent/broker? Did you research zoning, pending legislation, etc.?

Clearly, you can regroup since you have a six-figure income (assuming your living costs are reasonable), but as you move forward, vigilantly research your investment choices and carefully vet your advisors.

CONSIDER THE UPSIDES OF DEBT

HOUSE PURCHASE

If you want to buy a house, you are most likely going to need some financing. Without a mortgage loan, few people could make such a major acquisition. After all, it is the American dream. Home building remains a major driving force in the US economy, which affirms that the "dream" continues to be pursued.

CREDIT CARDS

Anyone who has ever had a critical incident, such as a car breaking down while traveling, can attest to the value of having a credit card on hand. In addition, you need not carry as much cash and you will receive a written accounting of your spending activities. And using the credit card and making timely payments builds one's credit worthiness. Sometimes there are even other benefits, such as discount reimbursement (cash back) and redeemable points for travel or merchandise. Also, if you have a problem with a retailer, the credit card company may act as your advocate.

AUTOMOBILES

A personal loan or auto financing to take advantage of a pricing opportunity, such as a deep discounted price on a new or used car, could make good sense. If there is a manufacturer's sale combined with dealer incentives, you may be able to save thousands on a new car. Many times those deals even include very low interest rates.

INVESTMENTS

Other times you may wish to borrow to take advantage of an investment opportunity. You may hear opportunity knocking, and you would like to answer the door. If you strongly believe in a secured, well-vetted opportunity—where you can earn an annual 18 percent or more return on an investment—then you may decide to borrow at a lower interest rate to recognize a net gain.

REST AND RELAXATION

Maybe you would like to take a much-needed, bargain-priced vacation. Sure, sometimes recreational and entertainment activities are a healthy move to refresh and rejuvenate. The current price may be attractive—whether your destination is Hawaii, Europe, Australia, Asia, Africa, or thirty miles down the road. If it is the right thing for you and you've saved almost enough to take the trip and a small loan is needed, then go for it, as long as the rest of your financial house is in order.

According to the Bureau of Labor Statistics, in 2013, the average spending for entertainment (defined as fees and admissions; audio and visual equipment and services; pets, toys, hobbies, playground equipment, and other services) was $2,482, or 4.9 percent of total household spending. In general, spending on entertainment increased with age, up to fifty-four years, and then declined. In terms of education levels, the share of spending on total entertainment went from 4.1 percent for those with less than a high school education to 5.2 percent for those with an associate's degree; it was 4.9 percent and 5.1 percent, respectively, for those with a bachelor's degree and those in the master's, professional, or doctoral degree category.[102]

EDUCATION

In many cases, education pays big dividends, so a college loan could be an excellent investment. For example, as mentioned in chapter 3, according to the US Bureau of Labor Statistics (2015), the median earnings for high school graduates are $35,256, and for college graduates with a bachelor's degree, the earnings are $59,124.

Getting Personal

Dear Drs. WDD and RVN,

I am a veteran with eight years of military service as an enlisted man in the US Marine Corps. I joined right after high school graduation. Now I am looking for a job and would like to build a successful future. My training and work in the corps was in communications. I am self-disciplined and eager to join the civilian workforce, but I'm not sure how to start.

I'd appreciate any suggestions.

Semper Fi

Dear Semper Fi,

First of all, thank you for your service. Our guess is that you are about twenty-six years old. Of course, communications is a huge spectrum, and you didn't specify which type of work you did in the Marine Corps. However, given your military experience, you may qualify for a position beyond an entry-level one, contingent on your prior training and work.

Did you take any courses while in the military? If so, such courses may qualify for transfer credit into a college degree program that connects with your background. Check with your local community college to see if your past training can be enhanced with a degree program. In all likelihood you are entitled to some financial assistance for a college degree, as well.

Your military experience coupled with a degree will greatly increase your chances to secure a job that is most fitting for you. Even if you initially take a job, you should consider working on a college degree on a part-time basis. There is a much higher probability of having a higher income and more job security with more education. So invest in yourself.

You may qualify for special consideration for jobs in both the public sector and the private sector. There are many programs available to assist vets to enter or reenter the civilian workforce.

After you are situated in a job, be sure to inquire into all assistance programs that exist for your career choice.

We wish you well in your pursuit.

CONSIDER THE DOWNSIDES OF DEBT

Liberal terms of credit acquisition will encourage excessive debt. If credit-granting standards are relaxed as they were during the 1990s and beyond, then more debt will be issued. With excessive borrowing by less credit-worthy debtors comes an increase in defaults.

Many borrowers were steered into mortgages that were too big for viable long-term debt service. Thus risk includes losing the home. Further, with current economic conditions, many find themselves in a situation where the mortgage on the house is greater than its market value. In other words, there is no equity. It is just a net liability. If the debt service is not sustainable, the ultimate result is foreclosure.

Too Much Debt May Lead to Late Payments

Poor payment practices can impact all interest rates for all credit sources. Read the small print. An example follows (in readable print!).

"If the promotional purchase rate was 1.99 percent and the rate for your other purchases was 16.99 percent and you pay late *once,* the rate for all purchases increases to 21.99 percent."

Once negative information goes into your credit-worthiness hopper, the interest rates on your credit cards and other forms of debt will most likely be hiked.

According to the Urban Institute, about 35 percent of adults with a credit file have a report of debt in collections. They owe an average of $5,178 (median $1,349). Debt in collections includes such liabilities as a credit card balance, medical bill, or utility bill that is more than 180 days past due.[103]

Excessive Impulsive Buying

Starting in the 1990s, not only was credit relatively easy to obtain, but we were strongly encouraged to use it. Credit became readily available for all purchases, including consumable products such as groceries, beverages, and, yes, even fast foods! In an age of focus on so much superficial spending, borrowing to indulge oneself is a decadent habit that creates yet another financial sinkhole. Such purchases are made without thought and are great for retailers, but they are not so great for consumers. Buying with debt will ultimately cost much more than the original purchase price.

RISKING CAPITAL

It seems your brother-in-law has just come up with another great idea to invest in. As he puts it, "It's a gold mine!" Well, maybe it's true, but whether you pump cash into the idea or just sign on as a partner, there is financial consequence. It may be good, bad, or downright ugly. You decide. Just remember, as a general partner, you are responsible for partnership debt. Be careful here, as you should be with any business investment.

Getting Personal

Dear Drs. WDD and RVN,

I have a wife and two kids, seven and four years old. Everyone is healthy and seems quite happy. My job is road maintenance for a small town. I earn enough to provide for the needs of my family, and we are satisfied with our lifestyle.

I have a chance to start a business of building outdoor wood furniture. I've been doing this for the past six years, and I am able to sell everything that I make. I like working with the wood, and everyone tells me I have talent. Should I take a chance of quitting my job and doing woodwork on a full-time basis? I don't like giving up my paycheck, and my wife thinks I should keep my day job.

Any help or thoughts would be appreciated.

Sawmill Bob

Dear Bob,

Good health and happiness, what a great combination!

It sounds like you are a true craftsman since you are able to sell everything you make. That's a large part of a business—the quality of the product itself.

However, if you enter this on a full-time basis, you must consider many more questions. Since you sell everything you make, the price must be fair to your customers, but is it fair to you? This is where business education should enter your life. A cost/volume/profit analysis is needed to determine if your selling price not only covers all costs but also generates a profit.

Other product matters must be analyzed. Where will you sell (in a store or shop)? Will you have a distributor? How will you promote or advertise your products, and what are the associated costs? What are your investment requirements for additional equipment, workshop space, and helpers to meet production needs?

Your wife is probably right. Keep your day job for now. Enroll in a business course. Helpful courses may include any that deal with small business start-ups, entrepreneurship, or marketing. Such courses will help you to learn a measureable approach to starting a business and will help to identify what is needed to achieve business sustainability. Nothing is risk free, but better business comprehension does increase the chance of success.

ARE YOU ENTREPRENEURIAL?

There are many points of view related to characteristics and classification of those who start a business. For example, according to Van Ness and Seifert, "Proactive entrepreneurs risk their own finances, career time, and professional reputation to establish, develop, and/or expand business ventures, which suggests an intense commitment to their business ventures. These are individuals for whom work is clearly a central focus compared to other business professionals."[104]

Studies indicate that entrepreneurs may be categorized within different groups: social entrepreneurs, student entrepreneurs, academic entrepreneurs, corporate entrepreneurs or intrapreneurs, and perhaps others.[105] Regardless of type of enterprise, there is no way to quantify who will become a successful entrepreneur. However, it is possible that with the right personal characteristics coalesced with an appropriate categorical environment an entrepreneurial spirit may emerge.

All things considered, and before becoming too enamored with the concept of self-employment, know that about half of all new establishments fail within five years, according to the Bureau of Labor Statistics.

To give further insight into prospective self-employment choices, the Bureau of Labor Statistics forecasts the fastest growing jobs through year 2022, coupled with the percent of self-employed participants.[106] More than half (51.4 percent) of landscaping and grounds keepers are self-employed. A large number, but still less than half (40.7 percent), of painting, construction, and maintenance jobs are held by the self-employed. Just a small fraction (6.7 percent) of accountants and auditors are self-employed. Of course, being self-employed requires many resources: a product or service that is truly needed, time, energy, creativity, expertise, entrepreneurial spirit, and capital. There are always pitfalls with any start-up business. Appropriate experience and education are essential to increase the likelihood of success.

Vignette: Tom G.

The outcome of the vignette that follows is quite similar to the hopes of Sawmill Bob.

Tom G., at fifty-two years old, decided to take early retirement from a major utility company. He lived very conservatively and accumulated substantial wealth. He was ready to leave his job of twenty-nine years. His true passion for work was found in his hobby-turned-small-business. He was an expert carpenter and enjoyed working with various woods to create custom-built furniture. Tom asked a management consultant friend to help him write a business plan. The plan revealed strong viability for a highly profitable business.

Tom moved forward with his business and maintained a large list of satisfied and repeat customers. Sales and profits exceeded his expectations.

In addition to working in his business, he donated time each month to teach high school kids who were in vocational education programs.

He found happiness in his new work life, and the money followed.

MAKE CAREFUL SPENDING CHOICES

As discussed in chapter 4, a basic need triggers a reaction when left unfulfilled. When you are hungry, no one needs to tell you. You feel it. The feeling may show up in different forms, such as stomach queasiness, angry abdominal growls, light-headedness, and edginess. Of course, physical reactions will also occur when in need of water. Needs are must-haves. Wants are things that we choose. Marketers are experts at sending us from our need states to our wants choices. Why else would we buy designer clothing to satisfy our need to cover our bodies? This blending of needs and wants applies to everything in life.

Consider Spending Reduction Issues and Viable Actions

Reduce credit card spending. Start by selecting the most vile account to pay off, and then stop using the targeted card. Search for lower interest rates with other companies. Use cash whenever possible. After you pay off one card balance, repeat the process.

Avoid impulse buying. Start focusing strictly on needs instead of wants. Remind yourself (and others) that logos and brand names are just a marketing ploy to siphon off more of your hard-earned money. Remind yourself that wearing logos is simply a proliferation of conspicuous consumption.

After reduction of credit card debt, what will you do with the extra cash? Pay off another credit card. Possibly open a savings account, even though interest rates are low. Cash accumulated may be used for emergencies or investment. Consider adding to a 401K or similar plan.

Consider downsizing or rightsizing with home ownership, or consider staying but refinancing at a lower rate. Carefully study current market conditions in your area. Do the math to be sure that there is a net gain. Discuss this matter with a reputable and competent realtor, bank, and/or financial advisor.

Vignette: Sea of Debt

Elaine M., forty-three years old, received an unexpected layoff notice on Friday, effective that day. She was told that she would be given six months' pay as a severance benefit. She was angry, embarrassed, and deeply hurt. Her reaction was to laugh it off and tell others that she would pick up another job with higher pay next week. She did not accept the reality of unemployment and continued to live normally without regard to the depletion of her savings. After all, from her frame of reference, it was a very poor move on the part of the company to lay her off, and they would pay for their mistake.

She was not able to find a job in the next month, nor in the next ten months because of her demand for high pay. She was caught in a spiral of decline where one bad situation led to another. Her cash assets were declining, and her self-esteem had bottomed out. Elaine allowed her ego to interfere with her pragmatism.

Indeed, behavior modification or compromise is, in many cases, a required part of life for overcoming adversity.

Getting Personal

Dear Drs. WDD and RVN,

Is there such a thing as a word to the wise or straightforward words of wisdom? If so, could such words help ensure finding prosperity?

Virginia

Dear Virginia,

The short answer to your questions is, yes, we believe so. We've collected some favorite words to live by as offered by satisfied millionaires from various interviews we have conducted. Although in random order, these words are food for thought as you move forward on the pathway to true prosperity. You will also note that these words generally convey a sense of optimism.

WORDS TO LIVE BY FROM SATISFIED MILLIONAIRES

Listen	Bargain hunt	Postpone
Negotiate	Sacrifice	Return stuff
Delay	Recycle	Substitute
Share	Borrow stuff	Compromise
Abbreviate	Economize	Abstain
Exercise	Compare	Quit smoking

Conserve	Frugality	Save
Courage	Self-discipline	Kindness
Pray	Be caring	Love
Friendly	Be polite	Think
Be understanding	Laugh	Honesty
Be reliable	Forget the Joneses	Life-long learning

REACHING TRUE PROSPERITY

BE CHARITABLE

There are no pockets in burial shrouds. So the options are to spend more, have it taxed away, give it to your children, and/or be charitable.

The *Oxford English Dictionary* explicitly defines charity in the first sense as Christian love, a word representing the Latin word *caritas* and the Greek word *agape*. Its applications include God's love of man and man's love of God and his neighbor, expressing itself in Christlike conduct. This is more fully described by St. Paul in 1 Corinthians 13. In this passage, St. Paul reminds us that emulating Christlike love is paramount: "If I have all faith so as to move mountains but do not have love, I am nothing. If I give away everything I own, and if I hand my body over so that I may boast but do not have love, I gain nothing." Acts of charity by mankind, in the first sense, are done for the love of God.

Secondary definitions without specific Christian associations define charity as love, kindness, affection, and benevolence to one's neighbors. It too is manifested through alms giving for the relief of the poor, irrespective of the motive, such as secular humanism.

This term—*charity*—is practically associated, in most cases, with the action of living by the Golden Rule.

The saying "Do unto others as you would have them do unto you" is rooted in the holy scriptures. In the New Testament, the gospel of Matthew tells us to be charitable.

- Do to others whatever you would have them do to you. (Matthew 7:12)

- You shall love your neighbor as yourself. (Matthew 19:19)

The Old Testament instructs us to

- give alms from your possessions (Tobit 4:7);

- give to the hungry some of your bread, and the naked some of your clothing (Tobit 4:16), and

- love your neighbor as yourself (Leviticus 19:18).

Combined, these represent a natural law, a moral conscience in the heart of all of us to do good.[107]

GIVING TIME AND MONEY

Putting words into action is critical to attaining happiness. This, of course, is done through time and money.

In the New Testament, James 2:14–17 asks: "What good is it, my brothers, if someone says he has faith but does not have works? Can that faith save him? If a brother or sister has nothing to wear and has no food for the day, and one of you says to them, 'Go in peace, keep warm, and eat well,' but you do not give them the necessities of the body, what good is it? So also faith of itself, if it does not have works, is dead."

AMERICA'S GENEROSITY

The Philanthropy Roundtable[108] provides important insights about America's generosity. Nearly three quarters (71 percent) of all charitable giving is from living donors. Two thirds (67 percent) of households give an average of 4 percent of their annual income for an average donation of $2,650. Conversely, one third of all households give nothing. Just one quarter (25 percent) of all adults volunteer their time. Of those who volunteer, they give on average 139 hours. The heavy givers of time and money can be described as married, well educated, Republican, and regular attenders of religious services.

Our data show that giving money to charity is positively related to life satisfaction. The more one gives, the more content one is. This relationship is shown in Figure 6-2.

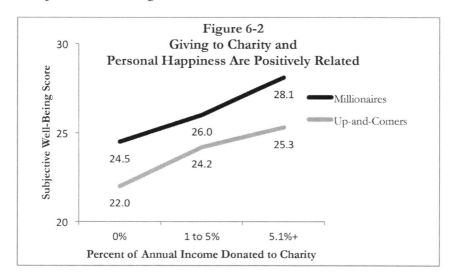

Figure 6-2
Giving to Charity and
Personal Happiness Are Positively Related

As was true for the discussion on the Golden Rule, the relationship between giving to charity and personal happiness is statistically significant.[109]

A minority of our survey respondents donate their time to others. Just 34 percent of the millionaires and 37 percent of the up-and-comers indicate that they enjoy volunteering. On average, up-and-comers give sixty-seven hours annually, and millionaires donate ninety-four hours. Of those who enjoy volunteering, however, personal happiness increases, as shown in Figure 6-3. Again, the relationship between volunteering and personal happiness is statistically significant.[110]

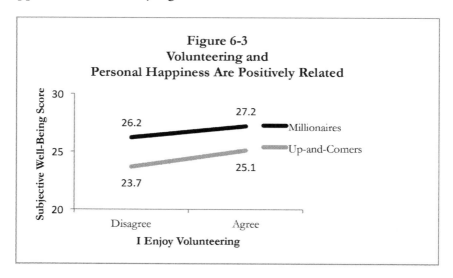

Figure 6-3
Volunteering and
Personal Happiness Are Positively Related

RELIGION

JEWS AND CHRISTIANS

There is no statistical difference between Jews and Christians regarding satisfaction, irrespective of net worth. In other words, slight differences in satisfaction can be attributed to chance in the measurement process; it is not systematic.

Millionaire Jews (n=58) indicated a satisfaction rating of 22.9 and millionaire Christians (n=438) had a rating of 24.2. Up-and-comers had a rating of 25.7 and 26.6 for satisfaction, respectively for Jews (n=119) and Christians (n=575).

GOD, ANXIETY, AND PEACE

Psalm 23—"The Lord is my shepherd"—contains but fifteen lines that, according to Rabbi Harold Kushner, can change your life for good.[111] In his short book, he dissects the psalm line by line, revealing the comfort it provides to those who are distressed, angry, or grieving. Indeed, it is one of the most frequently requested psalms at funerals. The promise of the prayer is that the Lord will restore our souls and that with Him, we will fear no evil. Practicing Christians and Jews alike truly find comfort in this scripture, for with God, we are never alone in our journey. And with God on our side, what else do we need for comfort?

As previously shown in Tables 5-3 and 5-4, the satisfied groups are more likely to make God central to their lives. The satisfied groups are less anxious about the future. The satisfied groups are more likely to be at peace with their souls. In Figure 6-4 we examine SWB scores for the overarching statement of "God is central to my life."

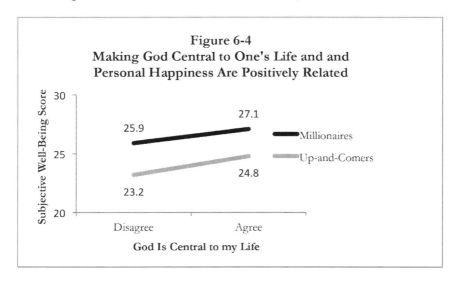

Figure 6-4
Making God Central to One's Life and and
Personal Happiness Are Positively Related

Those who make God central to their lives exhibit greater life satisfaction. The majority of millionaires (54.1 percent) indicated that God was central to their lives. They had an average satisfaction level of 27.1, whereas those who said He was not central had a score of 25.9, which was statistically lower. Likewise, the majority of up-and-comers (65.5 percent) agreed that God was central to their lives. They, too, had a statistically higher level of life satisfaction as compared to those who said that God was not central: 24.8 versus 23.2.[112]

Vignette: Happiness Found

Ron B., fifty-three years old, with no warning, was escorted from his desk to the parking lot. En route, the investment counselor was told that he was out of a job. Ron had many years of success in his field, and his net worth was $1.7 million. He earned very high commissions. However, over time, impossible sales goals were set by his manager that eventually led to his dismissal. Ron had a solid employment history as a seasoned financial professional and had volunteered countless hours for community development programs. He made generous donations to multiple charities. And now Ron was unemployed and distraught.

As a practicing Catholic, he was prayerful and through self-reflection felt that unemployment was just a temporary setback.

After consideration of his value system, he recognized that he would really like to work for an organization that helps people in need. Many of his volunteer hours were spent working for institutions such as the United Way. He had effectively raised funds for nonprofits and worked on community-development issues. He was a good team player and enjoyed planning and organizing. All things considered, he decided that he would like to manage a nonprofit organization. He pursued his interest and found an organization within his community that could benefit from his expertise and network connections.

The pay was less, but the work had much more appeal and much less stress. Ron is a satisfied millionaire.

THE PARABLE OF THE RICH FOOL: LUKE 12:16–20

There was a rich man whose land produced a bountiful harvest. He asked himself, "What shall I do, for I do not have space to store my harvest?"

And he said, "This is what I shall do: I shall tear down my barns and build larger ones. There I shall store all my grain and other goods and I shall say to myself, 'Now as for you, you have so many good things stored up for many years, rest, eat, drink, be merry!'"

But God said to him, "You fool, this night your life will be demanded of you; and the things you have prepared, to whom will they belong?"

Whether we believe in God or not, each of us must answer the question posed in the gospel of Luke: "And the things you have prepared, to whom will they belong?" This is a universal issue. Yet many will spend literally a lifetime acquiring things and more money, thinking that there is some magical amount and time when they can say, "Rest, eat, drink, be merry!"

Foolish, isn't it? There are those who have reached true prosperity and, of course, those who will. The essence of prosperity includes somewhat of a dilemma: How do such fortunate people plan for the future? This is the subject of chapter 7, the challenge of creating a dynasty.

BUILDING A DYNASTY

I have seen all things that are done under the sun, and
behold, all is vanity and a chase after wind.

—ECCLESIASTES 1:14

CAPRICIOUS WEALTH

Many smart people—physicians, lawyers, entrepreneurs—were defrauded by the biggest Ponzi scheme to date: the Madoff scandal.[113] Government investigators estimate losses of $50 billion. These smart investors will not be able to create a dynasty; there is nothing left to pass on. It seems that their plight is not much different from lucky lottery winners.

Consider three lottery winners who won great riches but were woefully unprepared to manage their wealth. These people won't be candidates to create a dynasty, either.

LOTTERY WINNERS: THREE TRAGIC LIVES

- Within a year of winning $16.2 million dollars in the 1988 Pennsylvania lottery, Bud Post found himself $1 million in debt. "Post has been involved in almost nonstop litigation since winning the jackpot. His landlady successfully sued him for a third of the prize, his sixth wife left him and his brother was jailed for trying to have him killed. In 1996, Post declared himself hexed and flat broke."[114] In 2006, Post died. In his words: "I won the lottery of death." He is survived by his seventh wife and nine children.[115]

- Suzanne Mullins failed to pay back a loan she obtained with her $4.2 million Virginia lottery winnings in 1993 used as collateral. In just eleven years after becoming a multimillionaire, she saw her fortune turn to debt. Despite winning a judgment against her, the finance company she borrowed from has yet to be repaid.[116]

- Janite Lee won an $18 million Illinois lottery in 1993, taking a lump sum payment of $5.9 million after taxes. In 2001, Lee found herself in US bankruptcy court in St. Louis, listing $1.8 million in assets and $2.5 million in debt.[117]

The lesson? These three lottery winners should have kept a low profile and not let their newfound riches change their lives in conspicuous ways.

KEEP A LOW PROFILE

Envious people can make the lives of lottery winners miserable—or worse. Others with great wealth can benefit by reflecting on their plight. Consider the physician we interviewed who enjoyed the finer things in life, including a valuable art collection in his home. Being prudent, he had a "professional" install an alarm system. To his surprise, it was the installer who later victimized him. Fortunately, he was able to recover his possessions, and the "professional" was arrested.

Even the highly wealthy share these problems, as Warren Buffett and his wife, Astrid, were once accosted in their own home![118] Here are two well-documented cases that further illustrate the potential problem of being able to enjoy your wealth in a conspicuous way.

Investment banker Edward S. Lampert was kidnapped in January 2003 while in a parking garage and held for a $1 million ransom. "Four hoodlums...targeted Lampert after a search for rich people on the Internet." He was released after a few days, and his captors were arrested and convicted.[119]

When Napoleon Beazley was seventeen, he and two of his friends were "looking for a vehicle to carjack...they caught sight of a cream-colored Mercedes-Benz, which they began to tail through a residential neighborhood of large, cantilevered houses and manicured lawns." During the commission of the carjacking, Beazley murdered an oil executive. At the age of twenty-five and out of appeals, he himself was executed in Texas.[120]

Members of the law enforcement community tell us that to avoid mayhem, one must keep a low profile. Assuming you do and you are able to avoid mayhem, how do you transfer your wealth to members of the next generation? Will they be prepared for the newfound tasks of good stewardship? This can be a vexing problem, given that three quarters of the millionaires surveyed expect to leave an inheritance.[121] So suppose you are able to enjoy your wealth and hope to preserve it. How have others succeeded (or not) in creating a dynasty? Before we consider methods of transferring wealth, why not become a "cryonaut" and never die?

BECOME A CRYONAUT

The *Wall Street Journal* estimates that there are perhaps one thousand "cryonauts"—those who hope to be "put on ice" at their death and then revived in the future to enjoy their appreciated assets. While this seems odd—and indeed medically improbable—financial institutions have been named as trustees to these so-called "revival trusts." As the *Journal* summarizes, "If they come back to life after being frozen, the funds revert back to them. Assuming, that is, there are no legal challenges to the plans."[122] A big *if.*

Possibly better solutions are to keep real estate in the family, pass on your wealth through a family business, or create a charitable foundation. Be certain to consult with a competent attorney specializing in elder law to ascertain the most-appropriate protection plan for your wishes in regard to the distribution of your estate. Keep in mind that estate updates are critical, especially related to financial status changes, births, deaths, divorces, marriages, health issues, and so on. A simple will may not be enough.

KEEP IT IN THE FAMILY WITH REAL ESTATE?

Our survey research shows that one third of the households with a net worth of at least $1 million hold investment real estate. Almost two thirds of the households with at least a $2.5 million net worth hold it as well. The trend is clear: those with greater wealth hold more real estate. However, transferring wealth through real estate is not necessarily sustainable, as the following historical account shows.

In the 1640s, Governor Peter Stuyvesant made a land grant of 1,500 acres in Flushing (Queens, part of New York City) to the Hallett family. Descendants who lived in this neighborhood signed the Declaration of Independence and fought in the Revolutionary War. Over the years, parcels were sold off, with the last piece sold by the family in the 1960s. In just over three hundred years, perhaps thirteen generations, one of the most valuable pieces of real estate in the world was no longer under one family's oversight.[123]

SUCCESSION PLANNING

Very often, wealth is created through entrepreneurial activity that creates a business entity. The Small Business Administration warns, however, that only one of three entities is successfully transferred to the second generation; only one in ten make it to the third.[124] Remarkably, here is an example of a company that has made it through four intergenerational transfers and 165 years: Southworth Paper Company headquartered in Massachusetts. President David C. Southworth, who answers to seventy family members, admits that "[a]fter five generations, you don't want to be the one to botch it up." [125] Well done, so far! Time will tell how long this will last. However, this longevity is a rare accomplishment. Consider the rise and fall of the Schwinn bicycle company.

CASE STUDY: SCHWINN[126]

In 1895, German machinist Ignaz Schwinn founded in Chicago the bicycle company that bears his name. With it, he had the dream of building the best bicycle the world had ever seen. Soon thereafter, there were more than three hundred bicycle manufacturers in the United States. He survived the competition of the time and often bought the assets of the bankrupt. He also built his manufacturing facilities in low-rent areas, to be even more competitive. Between 1900 and 1930, Schwinn bicycles held 14 percent of the market. Ignaz died in 1948.

In the 1920s, Ignaz established a trust, equally dividing the wealth among his children but giving the power to Frank W., his firstborn.

Ignaz's son, Frank W. (FW), "shared his father's appetite for the business." He made "swell" products; he negotiated tough deals with suppliers; he made the company prosper. "All told, Schwinn was awarded more than forty patents during the 1930s, while its annual production hit 346,000 units by 1941, more than twenty times what the company had sold just ten years earlier." FW died in 1963.

"FW's hard-driving ways and relatively simple lifestyle were a contrast to those of his sisters...They did what many heirs and heiresses do: they partied." By the mid-1950s, the company had annual sales of $25 million and a market share that slipped to 13.7 percent.

Frank V., FW's oldest son, assumed control of the business in 1963. "The V. stood for Valentine, and as the middle name suggests, he was about as different from dad as a son could get." In 1974, Frank V. suffered a heart attack and semiretired; earnings were $6.2 million on sales of $135 million. The company was becoming overstretched and had difficulty meeting demand, leaving Frank V. with no choice but to tell Schwinn dealers to "get bikes wherever you can." And at that, the mystique was lost; "power became even more diffused."

Schwinn no longer had a competitive edge of "made in America," foreign competition was fierce, and a sense of desperation consumed the company. When fourth-generation president, Edward R. Schwinn, Jr., asked his VP of finance what was needed in 1980, he jokingly replied: "An arsonist."

"Ed exhibited all the arrogance of a fourth-generation scion who was destined to be boss. One might say he was born with a silver spoke in his mouth. Heir to a dynasty whose business was a household name, he carried himself in the Schwinn vein—proud, stubborn, comfortable with the celebrity status—yet he possessed neither the drive of great-grandfather Ignaz nor the genius of his grandfather Frank W. Schwinn."

By 1992, "no savior was in sight. Schwinn was $75 million in debt, and losing $1 million a month." In the end, the fourteen remaining members of the Schwinn dynasty netted $2.5 million from the US bankruptcy court after the sale of company assets. Schwinn's "tumble is a saga of spectacular failure; of third- and fourth-generation family executives who lacked the passion to sustain their franchise."

The Schwinn story took four generations to develop. What follows is a success story that is still in progress.

A SUCCESS STORY (SO FAR): DAVE WORKS

Recently, we interviewed an industrious millionaire who is genuinely concerned about transferring his wealth to his children in a responsible manner. His name is Dave Works.

Dave had a difficult upbringing but was able to overcome obstacles, and he is currently worth $5 million. By his accounting, he is now richer than a millionaire in the truest sense.

While it is repulsive to think of one's father as Beelzebub, that is Dave's sentiment. From his father physically abusing his mother to not being recognized for the contributions he made to the family business, Dave felt cheated and alienated. But Dave points out, "When life gives you lemons, you have to make your own lemonade."

LIFE LESSONS LEARNED

Dave posed an interesting question: What does it mean to have a "successful" father? When Dave joined the family business, dropping out of college to do so, the firm had excellent production capabilities but no marketing abilities. Bringing marketing prowess into the mix, Dave grew sales from about $20,000 annually to $20 million by the end of his five-year tenure. His dad cashed out with $30 million and a new wife. Dave got nothing but a handshake and his ailing mother to care for.

This experience shaped Dave in important ways. He postponed his own marriage until he was thirty-three. Now over fifty and with two children (and still married to the same woman), Dave vows not to be like his "successful" father. This revelation came in 1993 after reflecting on a church sermon that convinced him that his earthly father is really secondary to his heavenly father. Dave had an epiphany. His priorities changed to focus on family and community.

Pursue Your Interests

Dave knows that life is short—too short to have hate in your heart, too short to be involved in litigation, and too short to have underperforming assets.

A real estate–dominated portfolio is most suited for Dave. He has no traded stocks or bonds, just $1 million in cash and $4 million in rental units, on which he enjoys a positive cash flow of $300,000 annually.

Dave's secret is that he is a hands-on, working manager. Since he does his own painting and drywall work, it makes sense for him to drive an old Chevy pickup truck to transport his tools and materials. As a working manager, and wanting to keep a low profile among his renters, he tells them that he is "just the manager." Complaints are handled in conference with his "directors," his Doberman.

The joy of self-employment is fulfilling. An added benefit is that he is able to get his sons actively involved in the business—it's a "bonding opportunity," he explains. Now he has forty rental units under management, his practical upper limit. He thought that he would stop with twenty, but his "innate drive, the challenge, the hunt" compelled him to continue.

Additional Considerations

A low profile and family bonding are important to Dave. He also embraces several other key strategies for successful property management. His advice:

- Don't be a flipper. Buy properties you are likely to keep for the life of a fifteen-year mortgage. The goose laying the golden eggs is an apt metaphor: fifteen years of rents (fresh eggs) is better than continually seeking new cash-flow opportunities (another goose).

- Preemptively evict before you rent to a deadbeat. Dave does this through a rigorous bullet-proof lease perfected over the years. For example, it includes restrictions against subletting, charges for visitors staying longer than seventy-two hours, a zero-tolerance drug policy, and a requirement that carpets be vacuumed weekly to minimize wear. Another landlord reviewed the lease, remarking that it was 99 percent in favor of the landlord. Dave asked his friend to point out the mistake he made regarding the other 1 percent. In sum, the lease has evolved over time and is the result of "having been ripped off a thousand times," says Dave.

- Work with heart and passion. Dave owns, manages, and repairs all of his properties. Nobody cares more about Dave's properties than Dave. As a result, the average stay of his renters is three years. The national average is eleven months. This stability adds to his profitability.

- Use the most-effective mechanism to protect your assets. Dave holds his properties in a family limited partnership (FLP). As a precaution, his properties are insured, but he has never had successful litigation against him. A potential plaintiff is told about the FLP. If there was a successful verdict beyond his insurance coverage, Dave's FLP would issue a 1099 to the winner, who would then be liable for taxes on the phantom income. This mechanism highlights Dave's aversion to litigation. It is far better to avoid it than to engage in it.

DAVE'S LEGACY

Dave is a success. He is healthy. He has a loving family. He is materially well-off. And his net worth is $5 million.

As he ages, he is hoping (and confident) that his children will embrace his version of quiet success. He does not seek public praise. The health and safety of his family are his highest priorities. "I am not fearful of death. If I can pass on the legacy of character and integrity to my children, if I can pass on the understanding that money is just a tool and not an end in itself, I'll consider myself a success," concludes Dave.

It seems as though Dave is doing the best he can do. But will his children's children have the same interest and drive? Perhaps creating a carefully structured charitable foundation is the answer, where family members can be employed for generations.

CREATE A CHARITABLE FOUNDATION?

There are at least three motives why one would want to create a charitable foundation: leave a personal family legacy, engage the family in philanthropy, and receive tax deductions. However, creating a foundation for future generations to manage may not be prudent. Consider that the F. W. Olin Foundation closed fifty-four years after the death of its founder, Franklin.[127] The John M. Olin Foundation (John was Franklin's son) dissolved after thirty years of activity, spending itself out of existence, as planned. The reason for closing is clear in both cases. Quoting New York philanthropist Peter Flanigan: "Perpetual foundations are quite silly. They exist for the benefit of trustees and staff rather than for the goals set forth by the original donor." [128] Despite prudent planning, the Knott and Carvel families might have benefited by taking this advice.

Knott Family

In an unfortunate case, good intentions ended in litigation for the closely knit Knott family over the distribution of money. After the death of the patriarch in 1995 but before the death of his wife in 2003, millions of dollars were donated to charities directly, instead of through the family's charitable foundation. While the courts ruled this to be a premature distribution, one could argue that the administrators were acting on the father's moral philosophy. Clearly, the father was very charitable during his lifetime. One of his daughters recalled in 2003 what her father thought: "Those who are rich in world goods should not be proud and should not rely on so uncertain a thing as wealth. They should do good, be rich in good deeds sharing what they have." These words were taken to heart by the administrators of his estate (but before his wife died), literally "sharing what they have" with worthy causes, instead of adding to the endowment of the family's foundation. Eventually the foundation would receive the remainder of the estate, as expressed in their wills.[129] It seems that Mr. Knott inadvertently caused the problem himself by expressing sentiments that may have been contrary to legal requirements.

Carvel Ice Cream

Tom Carvel created a chain of 850 ice cream shops and left an estate valued at $67 million when he died in 1990. Over the next eighteen years, the fight over its distribution continued among his lawyer, his secretary, his charity, his widow, and his niece. "By any measure, the case is a legal colossus. More than forty lawyers have had a hand in the litigation. Legal fees and commissions have already drained more than $28 million from the Carvel fortune."[130] This drama could have been avoided, according to one analyst, had Mr. Carvel purchased an annuity for his wife from an insurance company, and willing his estate to charity. Instead, he made bequests to 83 different beneficiaries, complicating his estate. [131]

BUFFETT'S SOLUTION

Warren Buffett, one of world's richest men, says: "I want to give my kids just enough so that they would feel they could do anything but not so much that they would feel like doing nothing."[132]

So what will become of Buffett's fortune? He's giving it to charity. The majority is going to the Bill and Melinda Gates Foundation, already the world's largest.[133] And to ensure that the foundation stays true to its current mission, the Gates Foundation will spend itself out of existence fifty years after the death of its current trustees.[134]

CHAPTER 8

Final Thoughts

HAVE A PURPOSE GREATER THAN YOURSELF

After reading this book, it should be clear that you are responsible for your own choices, actions and results. It is possible to be rich and miserable. It is also entirely possible to have a modest financial net worth, and yet have high life satisfaction. Which actions offered in this book will you take to strengthen your chances to be rich and happy?

One casual piece of advice we hear from pop psychologists is to follow your dreams. While seemingly liberating, it is content free advice. After all, how will you support yourself? (Recall the advice to work for money while young and to live off your net worth when old.) Even highly paid athletes, physicians, and executives can't work forever. Without a commitment to saving and investing, how will you afford retirement?

We trust that our research-based guidance is better: follow a worthy dream that allows for a sustainable lifestyle. This will allow you to avoid being a captain of a ship without a rudder.

Marketers are very good about offering you the next new thing that will change your life. Before you embrace their message, ask yourself what you value most. Which choices will you act on? Do you need a new car or will a used (and depreciated) one be sufficient? Do you really want to get excited about the first ding you get in a parking lot? Do you need to select an expensive school, or do you realize that your personal effort is more important as a determinant of success? And how about a house? Do you need one with a wall-to-wall mortgage? Do you really need to impress anyone?

The vignettes, letters and survey research we presented provide a pathway to true prosperity that can make you far richer than a millionaire. In all likelihood behavior modification will be required. And change is hard. Benjamin Franklin understood this, as he concluded in *The Way to Wealth* essay 250 years ago: the people heard the advice, agreed with it, and then practiced the contrary.

We must develop a worthy action plan and then implement it. The choices, actions, and results are up to you. To this end, consider the advice from Auschwitz survivor and psychiatrist Viktor Frankl:[135]

Don't aim at success—the more you aim at it and make it a target, the more you are going to miss it. For success, like happiness, cannot be pursued; it must ensue, and it only does so as the unintended side effect of one's personal dedication to a cause greater than oneself…listen to what your conscience commands you to do and go carry it out to the best of your knowledge.

Change is difficult, but in the United States of America we have an environment that allows for change. Consider the wisdom from the late economists Milton and Rose Friedman in their book *Free to Choose*:

A society that puts equality—in the sense of equality of outcome—ahead of freedom will end up with neither equality nor freedom. The use of force to achieve equality will destroy freedom, and the force, introduced for good purposes, will end up in the hands of people who use it to promote their own interests.

On the other hand, a society that puts freedom first will, as a happy by-product, end up with both greater freedom and greater equality. Though a by-product of freedom, greater equality is not an accident. A free society releases the energies and abilities of people to pursue their own objectives. It prevents some people from arbitrarily suppressing others. It does not prevent some people from achieving positions of privilege, but so long as freedom is maintained, it prevents those positions of privilege from becoming institutionalized; they are subject to continued attack from other able, ambitious people. Freedom means diversity but also mobility. It preserves the opportunity for today's disadvantaged to become tomorrow's privileged and, in the process, enables almost everyone, from top to bottom, to enjoy a fuller and richer life.[136]

In brief, we are all free to change and to choose a purpose greater than ourselves. But the question is: will you exercise that freedom?

RECOMMENDED READING

As educators, we know we can never learn enough. While we made reference to many studies, there are more to consider. Please allow us to recommend some books that have shaped our thinking about building wealth.

The Richest Man In Babylon (1926) by George S. Clason is a short parable that is called the most inspiring book on wealth ever written. That's quite a claim, but it does show that the laws for wealth building applicable six thousand years ago hold true today.

The success of Andrew Carnegie inspired Napoleon Hill to write *Think & Grow Rich* (1937). Particularly useful is the section of fifty-five famous alibis by old man If—if I had more time, if I had money, if I lived in a big city, if I were not fat, and so on. These ghosts of fear can be destroyed by studying Hill's book. This book will also show you how to develop persistence and how to surround yourself with wise people.

Princeton economics professor Burton G. Malkiel's *A Random Walk Down Wall Street* (1973) book has been revised periodically. With thousands of sources for investment advice available to all of us, it is easy to get confused. The good professor lays out a plan for managing a diversified set of investments over a lifetime, paying particular attention to risk tolerance. This could be the only investment guide you need.

It is personally rewarding to donate your time as a volunteer, no matter what your financial wealth is. But money certainly helps to fund causes in this material world. Professor Arthur C. Brooks's book about **Who Really Cares** (2006) shows that compassionate conservatism is an important driving force in America. He shows through extensive survey work that giving money to charity speaks louder than just talking about caring. He argues successfully, in our view, that charitable Americans improve life for all of us and selfish Americans make us all worse off.

APPENDIX

SAMPLE CHARACTERISTICS

We designed and funded our own survey of high net worth households. Two separate samples of US homeowners with annual incomes of $100,000 or more were combined into one usable sample. One sample of ten thousand households was sent a questionnaire without an incentive. Another set of five thousand included a dollar bill with the questionnaire. Details are shown in Table A-1.

Table A-1
Survey Response Rate

Questionnaire with....	Mailed Out	Undeliverable	Unusable	Usable Sample	Response Rate*
No Incentive	10,000	78	29	606	6.4%
$1 Enclosed	5,000	42	122	840	19.4%
Totals	15,000	120	151	1,446	10.7%

* Response Rate = (Usable + Unusable) / (Mailed Out – Undeliverable)

NB: Using a paper clip to attach $1 to the questionnaire triples the response rate.

Tables A-2 and A-3 provide details about the geographic, gender, age, education, employment, and political affiliation of the sample by net worth.

Table A-2
Geographic, Gender, and Age Distribution
of Sample by Net Worth

	Household Net Worth	
	Less than $1,000,000	$1,000,000 or More
First Zip Code Digit & State, DC	n=	n=
0 = CT MA ME NH NJ RI VT	33	67
1 = DE NY PA	54	66
2 = DC MD NC SC VA WV	75	67
3 = AL FL GA MS TN	81	103
4 = IN KY MI OH	94	97
5 = IA MN MT ND SD WI	28	29
6 = IL KS MO NE	83	85
7 = AR LA OK TX	64	93
8 = AZ CO ID NM NV UT WY	34	37
9 = AK CA HI OR WA	79	145
Unknown Zip Code	12	20

Gender		
Female	229	163
Male	408	646

Age		
20-29	4	1
30-39	51	14
40-49	230	225
50-59	249	376
60-69	65	137
70-79	29	41
80+	9	13
Unknown	0	2

Table A-3
Education, Employment Status, and Political Affiliation
of Sample by Net Worth

	Household Net Worth	
	Less than $1,000,000	$1,000,000 or More
Education Completed	n=	n=
Less than high school	1	2
High school graduate	11	12
Vocational / technical school	5	6
Some college	107	56
Four-year college graduate	234	293
Master's degree	170	260
Law school graduate	45	73
Medical school graduate	23	57
Dental school graduate	7	16
Other health doctorate	6	7
Academic doctorate	28	27
Employment Status		
Self-employed	162	261
Corporate employment	213	216
Public sector employment	79	33
Professional practice	78	89
Retired / disabled	63	154
Unemployed, seeking work	18	19
Unemployed, not seeking work	4	5
Homemaker	20	31
Unknown	0	1
Political Affiliation		
Republican	289	438
Democrat	178	171
Independent	70	89
Other	8	6
None	92	105

NOTES

1. James MacLachlan, "Making a Message Memorable and Persuasive," *Journal of Advertising Research* 23, no. 6 (1983): 51–59.

2. All biblical references are from: <u>The New American Bible</u>, Saint Joseph Edition, Catholic Book Publishing Corp, 1992.

3. Carol Nickerson, Norbert Schwarz, Ed Diener, and Daniel Kahneman, "Zeroing In On the Dark Side of the American Dream: A Closer Look at the Negative Consequences of the Goal for Financial Success," *Psychological Science* 14, no. 6 (2003): 531–36.

4. See Ed Diener, Robert A. Emmons, Randy J. Larsen, and Sharon Griffin, "The Satisfaction with Life Scale," *Journal of Personality Assessment* 49, no. 1 (1985): 71–75; and William Pavot and Ed Diener, "Review of the Satisfaction with Life Scale," *Psychological Assessment* 5, no. 2 (1993): 164–172.

5. Betsey Stevenson and Justin Wolfers, "Subjective Well-Being and Income: Is There Any Evidence of Satiation?" (working paper, Centre for Applied Macroeconomic Analysis, Crawford School of Public Policy, the Australian National University, 2013).

6. Thomas J. Stanley and William D. Danko, *The Millionaire Next Door* (Atlanta: Longstreet Press, 1996).

7. Do a Google search on "The Way to Wealth." This 3,500-word essay was written by Benjamin Franklin in 1758 under the pseudonym Richard Saunders (as in *Poor Richard's Almanac*).

8. Richard Leifer, Christopher M. McDermott, Gina Colarelli O'Connor, Lois S. Peters, Mark Rice, and Robert W. Veryzer, *Radical Innovation— How Mature Companies Can Outsmart Upstarts* (Boston: Harvard Press, 2000), 157.

9. John Naber, comp., *Awaken the Olympian Within* (Torrance, California: Griffin Publishing Group, 1999), 136.

10. www.forbes.com/profile/james-dyson/

11. Sources: www.dolby.com, www.famousinventors.org/ray-dolby, and Marcus Williamson (13 September 2013) Ray Dolby obituary, *The Independent*. (DLB value as of 8/29/17)

12. Issie Lapowsky (July, August 2013) "9 Questions for Angie Hicks," *Inc. Magazine*. (ANGI value as of 8/29/17).

13. Regina Schrambling (18 April 2002), "Ruth Fertel of Steakhouse Fame Is Dead at 75," *New York Times*. (RUTH value as of 8/29/17).

14. N. Gregory Mankiw, "Fair Taxes? Depends What You Mean by 'Fair,'" *New York Times*, July 15, 2007.

15. Glen Johnson, "Heinz Kerry Paid $750,000 in Taxes," *Boston Globe*, May 12, 2004.

16. 2nd Court of Appeals Judge Learned Hand in his decision on Helvering v. Gregory, 69 F.2d 809, 810-11 (2d Cir. 1934).

17. Marc Weingarten, "Leonard Cohen's Troubles May Be a Theme Come True," *New York Times*, October 6, 2006.

18. Alan Kohler, "Hey, That's No Way to Say Good-bye," *Sydney Morning Herald* (Australia), October 4, 2006.

19. Sean Michaels, "Leonard Cohen's Ex-manager Sentenced to 18 Months in Jail," *Guardian*, April 19, 2012.

20. Mr. Micawber from Charles Dickens's *David Copperfield* (1850).

21. Richard J. Van Ness and Edith M. Donohue, *Life after Layoff* (Albany: Whitston Publishing, 2003), 131.

22. Board of Governors of the Federal Reserve System, *Report to the Congress on the Profitability of Credit Card Operations of Depository Institutions* (Washington, DC, 2016).

23. Charlotte A. Schoenborn, M.P.H., Division of Health Interview Statistics, "Marital Status and Health: United States, 1999-2002," Number 351, December 15, 2004

24. Stephen King, *On Writing* (New York: Scribner, 2000), 154.25

25. Kenneth R. Fox, "The Influence of Physical Activity on Mental Well-Being," *Public Health Nutrition* 2, no. 3a (1999): 411–418.

26. Amy Stevens, "Somber Reunion for Harvard Law's Class of '85," *The Wall Street Journal*, May 8, 1995: B1.

27. Stacy Berg Dale and Alan B. Krueger, "Estimating the Payoff of Attending a More Selective College," *The Quarterly Journal of Economics*, November 2002, pages 1491-1527.

28. See BLS.gov for historical data.

29. http://articles.moneycentral.msn.com/RetirementandWills/EscapeTheRatRace/JustHow RichIsRichReally.aspx

30. Tom Sullivan, "Are You Rich?," *Barron's Online*, March 18, 2008.

31. See the appendix for details about the survey research.

32. The data set includes several respondents with a $20 million net worth. Their multiplier is 1.4, meaning that to feel rich, they "need" $28 million. For those with a $100,000 net worth, the multiplier is 20, so $2 million is "needed" to feel rich.

33. https://www.ssa.gov/policy/docs/chartbooks/fast_facts/2015/fast_facts15.pdf

34. "Wages and salaries were 92 percent of income before taxes for consumers ages 25 to 34 in 2014," *The Economics Daily*, Bureau of Labor Statistics, US Department of Labor, accessed June 28, 2016, https://www.bls.gov/opub/ted/2016/wages-and-salaries-were-92-percent-of-income-before-taxes-for-consumers-ages-25-to-34-in-2014.htm

35. "Where Is the Wealth of Nations?" (Washington, DC: The World Bank, 2006).

36. "Global Migration Barometer," (Western Union and Economist Intelligence Unit), August 2008.

37. $rate = \sqrt[379\ years]{\dfrac{\$186{,}000{,}000{,}000}{\$24}} - 1 = 6.19\% / year$

38. Barbara Stewart, "Carol Hochberg, 40, Advocate for Victims of Breast Cancer," *New York Times*, September 20, 1998.

39. Richard Gibson, "Bain Capital Pays Estimated $1 Billion For 90%-Plus Stake in Domino's Pizza," *Wall Street Journal*, September 28, 1998.

40. Benjamin Pimentel, "Lingerie Firm Founder Dies—Body in Bay—Former Victoria's Secret Owner Left Car at Bridge," *San Francisco Chronicle*, September 1, 1993; and Michael J. Ybarra, "Roy Raymond's Life and Death Yield Grim Case Study," *Wall Street Journal*, September 29, 1993.

41. Edwin Arlington Robinson, *Collected Poems* (London: Cecil Palmer, 1922), 82.

42. "Changes in US Family Finances from 2010–2013," *Federal Reserve Bulletin* 100, no. 4 (2014): 1-41.

43. The US Census Bureau and the Federal Reserve use the terms *families* and *households* interchangeably.

44. "How Many Millionaires? Depends Who's Counting," Robert Frank, CNBC, accessed August 17, 2017, https://www.cnbc.com/2015/06/24/how-many-millionaires-in-the-world-it-depends.html.

45. In the longitudinal (1972–2014) General Social Survey from the University of Chicago, happiness was measured as follows: "Taken all together, how would you say things are these days, would you say that you are very happy, pretty happy, or not too happy?" In 1972 17.2 percent of adults were not too happy, and in 2014 the number was 12.2 percent.

46. Martha Stout, *The Sociopath Next Door: The Ruthless Versus the Rest of Us* (New York: Broadway Books, 2005).

47. Board of Governors of the Federal Reserve System, *Report on the Economic Well-Being of US Households in 2014.* https://www.federalreserve.gov/econresdata/2014-report-economic-well-being-us-households-201505.pdf

48. Board of Governors ofthe Federal Reserve System, Federal Reserve Bulletin, September 2017, Vol. 103, No. 3.

49. Mike Patton, "US Health Care Costs," Forbes.com, accessed June 29, 2015, https://www.forbes.com/forbes/welcome/?toURL=https://www.forbes.com/sites/mikepatton/2015/06/29/u-s-health-care-costs-rise-faster-than-inflation/&refURL=https://www.google.com/&referrer=https:/

50. "National Health Expenditure Projections 2015–2025," Centers for Medicare and Medicaid Services, accessed February 2, 2015, https://www.cms.gov/Newsroom/MediaReleaseDatabase/Press-releases/2017-Press-releases-items/2017-02-15-2.html

51. Stephanie Armour, "ACA Premiums Jump 25%; "Administration Acknowledges Extended Enrollment", *Wall Street Journal*, October 25, 2016.

52. Ann C. Foster, "Household healthcare spending in 2014," Bureau of Labor Statistics Beyond the Numbers 5, no. 13 (August 2016).

53. Richard J. Van Ness and Edith M. Donohue, *Life after Layoff* (Albany: Whitston Publishing, 2003), 36.

54. Claudia Sahm, "Deleveraging: Is It Over and What Was It?", FEDS Notes, accessed June 24, 2014, https://www.federalreserve.gov/

econresdata/notes/feds-notes/2014/deleveraging-is-it-over-and-what-was-it-20140624.html

55. Financial Accounts of the United States, 2015.

56. Richard J. Van Ness and Edith M. Donohue, *Life after Layoff* (Albany: Whitston Publishing, 2003), 36.

57. See, for example, books by David Bach, such as *Automatic Millionaire* (New York: Crown Business 2005), and *Start Late Finish Rich* (New York: Broadway 2007), or by Brian Tracy, such as *21 Success Secrets of Self-Made Millionaires* (San Francisco: Berrett-Koehler 2001), *Million-Dollar Habits* (Entrepreneur Press 2004), and *Getting Rich Your Own Way* (Hoboken, NJ: John Wiley and Sons 2004).

58. Louis Rukeyser, *Book of Lists* (New York: Henry Holt and Company, 1997): 101–103.

59. Keith Bradsher, "For Most US Households, Inheritances Hardly Count," *New York Times*, July 25, 1995. The report is based on the Rand study "Unequal Wealth and Incentives to Save," by James P. Smith, DB-145-RC.

60. Angus Deaton, "Policy Implications of the Gradient of Health and Wealth; An Economist Asks, Would Redistributing Income Improve Population Health?" *Health Affairs*, March/April 2002.

61. James Q. Wilson, *The Marriage Problem: How Our Culture Has Weakened Families* (New York: Harper Collins, 2002), 16.

62. Linda J. Waite and Maggie Gallagher, *Marriage: Why Married People Are Happier, Healthier, and Better Off Financially* (New York: Doubleday, 2000).

63. Sharon Jayson, "U of C Sociologist: Divorce Can Be Hazardous to Your Health," *Chicago Sun Times*, June 28, 2005.

64. Laura Meckler, "How a US Official Promotes Marriage to Fight Poverty," *Wall Street Journal*, November 20, 2006.

65. Danny G. Blanchflower and Andrew J. Oswald, "Money, Sex and Happiness: An Empirical Study," special issue, *Scandinavian Journal of Economics* (2004).

66. Eric Dash, "Sex May Be Happiness, but Wealth Isn't Sexiness," *New York Times*, July 11, 2004.

67. Joseph Lupton and James P. Smith, "Marriage, Assets, and Savings" (working paper series 99-12, DRU-2215-NICHD, Rand, 1999), 25.

68. Thomas J. Stanley and William D. Danko, *The Millionaire Next Door* (Atlanta: Longstreet Press, 1996), 3.

69. John P. Kotter, *The New Rules: How to Succeed in Today's Post-corporate World* (New York: The Free Press, 1995). See especially Exhibits 2.4, 2.5, and 8.4 and footnotes 17 and 18 for chapter 8.

70. Ana M. Aizcorbe, Arthur B. Kennickell, and Kevin B. Moore, "Recent Changes in US Family Finances: Evidence from the

1998 and 2001 Survey of Consumer Finances," Federal Reserve Bulletin, January. See especially table 3. In 1992, the ratio of average financial net worth was 1:4.9 for working for someone else versus being self-employed; in 1995, the ratio was 1:5.2; in 1998 it was 1:5.5; and in 2001, the ratio was 1:5.6.

71. Abraham Maslow, *Motivation and Personality*, 2nd ed. (New York: Harper & Row, 1987).

72. Geert Hofstede, "The Cultural Relativity of the Quality of Life Concept," *Academy of Management Review* 9, no. 3 (1984): 389–98.

73. "High-Income Households Spent Half of Their Food Budget on Food Away from Home in 2015," *The Economics Daily*, Bureau of Labor Statistics, US Department of Labor, accessed October 5, 2016, https://www.bls.gov/opub/ted/2016/high-income-households-spent-half-of-their-food-budget-on-food-away-from-home-in-2015.htm

74. Beverage Marketing Corporation, accessed March 16, 2017, www.beveragemarketing.com/news-detail.asp?id=389.

75. Abraham Maslow, *Motivation and Personality*, 2nd ed. (New York: Harper & Row, 1987).

76. "FBI Releases 2015 Crime Statistics", National Press Office, Department of Justice and Federal Bureau of Investigation, September 26, 2016, https://www.fbi.gov/news/pressrel/press-releases/fbi-releases-2015-crime-statistics

77. National Center for Health Statistics, Health, United States, 2015, Table 19, https://www.cdc.gov/nchs/data/hus/hus15.pdf

78. Edward Hoffman, *The Right to Be Human: A Biography of Abraham Maslow* (New York: McGraw Hill, 1999).

79. E. Laird Landon, "Self-Concept, Ideal Self-Concept, and Consumer Purchase Intentions," *Journal of Consumer Research* 1, no. 2 (1974): 44–51.

80. Abraham Maslow, *Towards a Psychology of Being,* 3rd ed. (New York: John Wiley & Sons, 1999).

81. Abraham Maslow, *Motivation and Personality*, 2nd ed. (New York: Harper & Row, 1987).

82. National Center for Health Statistics, United States, 2015, (Data are for 2014), https://www.cdc.gov/nchs/data/hus/hus15.pdf

83. Mark Lino , Kevin Kuczynski, Nestor Rodriguez, TusaRebecca Schap, "Expenditures on Children by Families," 2015, USDA, Center for Nutrition Policy and Promotion, Misc. Report, Revised March 2017.

84. Jim Holt, "Against Happiness," *New York Times*, June 20, 2004.

85. Ed Diener, "Subjective Well-Being: The Science of Happiness and a Proposal for a National Index," *American Psychologist* 55, no. 1 (2000): 34–43.

86. David G. Myers and Ed Diener, "Who Is Happy?" *Psychological Science* 6, no. 1 (1995): 10–19.

87. Toksoz Byram Karasu, *The Spirit of Happiness* (New York: Simon & Schuster, 2006).

88. Farr A. Curlin, et. al. (2007), "The Relationship Between Psychiatry and Religion Among U.S. Physicians," Psychiatric Services, September, Vol. 58, No. 9, pages 1193-1198.

89. Farr A. Curlin, et. al. (2007), "Religion, Spirituality, and Medicine: Psychiatrists' and Other Physicians' Differing Observations, Interpretations, and Clinical Approaches," American Journal of Psychiatry, December, Vol. 164, No. 12, pages 1825-1831.

90. Conference presentation by psychiatrist Marilyn Baetz reported by Greg Basky in the news and analysis section of the Canadian Medical Association Journal (CMAJ), November 28, 2000; 163 (11), page 1497.

91. Aristotle, *Nicomachean Ethics*, 5th rev. ed., trans. W. D. Ross (Oxford: Oxford University Press, 1949), section 1097b. See also Mortimer J. Adler, *Aristotle for Everybody: Difficult Thought Made Easy* (New York: Macmillan, 1978).

92. Dean Alfange, "Words to live by: A message for nineteen fifty-two, My Creed," *This Week* magazine section from *The Sunday Bulletin*, Philadelphia, December 30, 1951, page 2.

93. Ed Diener, Robert A. Emmons, Randy J. Larsen, and Sharon Griffin, "The Satisfaction with Life Scale," *Journal of Personality Assessment* 49, no. 1 (1985): 71–75.

94. Where 1 = strongly disagree, 2 = disagree, 3 = slightly disagree, 4 = neither agree nor disagree, 5 = slightly agree, 6 = agree, and 7 = strongly agree.

95. William Pavot and Ed Diener, "Review of the Satisfaction with Life Scale," *Journal of Psychological Assessment* 5, no. 2 (1993): 164–72.

96. Examining the entire sample, the Pearson correlation between subjective well-being and the seven-point scale about feeling anxious about the future, where lower scores represent higher agreement, is –.29, with p < .000.

97. See Luke 12:16–20.

98. Sumit Agarwal, Vyacheslav Mikhed, and Barry Scholnick, "Does Keeping Up with the Joneses Cause Financial Distress? Evidence from Lottery Winners and Neighboring Bankruptcies" (working paper 16-04/R, https://ssrn.com/abstract=2731562, 2016).

99. For millionaires, p(F=23.07 with 1/795 df)=.0000; and for up-and-comers, p(F=32.26 with 1/555 df)=.0000.

100. These quotes are from https://goodreads.com.

101. Erin El Issa, 2016 American Household Credit Card Debt Study, https://www.nerdwallet.com/blog/average-credit-card-debt-household/ and Patricia Buckley 10/30/2014, The dismal state of consumer finances (Deloitte University Press) https://dupress.deloitte.com/dup-us-en/economy/behind-the-numbers/consumer-finances-and-retirement.html

102. Office of Prices and Living Conditions, "Consumer spending on entertainment by household income in 2013," Bureau of Labor Statistics, *Beyond the Numbers* 4, no. 6 (May 2015).

103. Caroline Ratcliffe, Signe-Mary McKernan, Brett Theodos, and Emma Cancian Kalish, Research Report, Urban Institute, July 29, 2014.

104. Raymond Van Ness and Charles Seifert, "A Theoretical Analysis of the Role of Characteristics in Entrepreneurial Propensity," *Strategic Entrepreneurship Journal* 10 (2016): 89–96.

105. Ibid.

106. "Self-Employment: What to Know to Be Your Own Boss," Dennis Vilorio, Bureau of Labor Statistics, accessed June 2014, https://www.bls.gov/careeroutlook/2014/article/self-employment-what-to-know-to-be-your-own-boss.htm

107. Catechism of the Catholic Church, paragraph 1776, Article 6: Moral Conscience.

108. Karl Zinmeister, *The Almanac of American Philanthropy* (Washington, DC: The Philanthropy Roundtable, 2016).

109. For millionaires, p(F=16.73 with 2/770 df)=.0000, and for up-and-comers, p(F=5.67 with 2/538 df)=.0037.

110. For millionaires, p(F=6.82 with 1/795 df)=.0092, and for up-and-comers, p(F=7.54 with 1/555 df)=.0062.

111. Harold S. Kushner, *The Lord Is My Shepherd* (New York: Anchor Books, 2004).

112. For millionaires, p(F=10.06 with 1/795 df)=.0016, and for up-and-comers, p(F=10.22 with 1/555 df)=.0015.

113. Stephen Gandel, "The Madoff Fraud: How Culpable Were the Auditors?," *Time*, http://www.time.com/time/business/article/0,8599,1867092,00.html.

114. Patrick Hernan, "Lotto Winner, Arrested, Faces Extradition," *Pittsburgh Post-Gazette*, August 13, 1998.

115. Moustafa Ayad, "William Post III; April 5, 1939 to January 15, 2006; Lottery Winner Whose Wealth Brought Grief, Troubled Times," *Pittsburgh Post Gazette*, January 18, 2006.

116. Laurence Hammack, "Roanoke Lottery Winner Hears Price She Must Pay," *Roanoke Times*, May 3, 2004.

117. Jim Gallagher, "Court Begins Figuring Out Bankruptcy of $18 Million Lottery Winner; Janite Lee's Lawyer Faults Big Loans, Gambling," *St. Louis Post-Dispatch*, September 11, 2001.

118. M. P. McQueen, "Wave of Home Invasions Puts the Wealthy on Alert," *Wall Street Journal*, November 15, 2007.

119. Robert Berner and Susann Rutledge, "The Next Warren Buffett?" *Business Week* 3909, November 22, 2004.

120. Pamela Colloff, "Does Napoleon Beazley Deserve to Die?," *Texas Monthly*, April 2002; and Pamela Colloff, "Napoleon's Last Stand," *Texas Monthly*, July 2002.

121. Based on a sample of 797 millionaire homeowners, 22.5 percent agreed that "I hope to die broke, spending most of my money before I die."

122. Antonio Regalado, "A Cold Calculus Leads Cryonauts to Put Assets on Ice," *Wall Street Journal*, January 21, 2006.

123. Robert F. Worth, "Blue Blood at the Gas Pumps; Queens Families Still Have Their Legacy, if Not Their Land," *New York Times*, January 3, 2004.

124. http://sba.gov/library/pubs/eb-1.pdf

125. Trudy Tynan, "Family Paper Firm Now into Fifth Generation," Associated Press State & Local Wire, August 1, 2004.

126. This section is based on the 350-page book by Judith Crown and Glenn Coleman, *No Hands: The Rise and Fall of the Schwinn Bicycle Company, an American Institution* (New York: Henry Holt and Company, 1996).

127. Debra E. Blum, "Closing the Doors at a Big Philanthropy," *Chronicle of Philanthropy*, April 14, 2005.

128. "Parting Gift," *Wall Street Journal*, April 23, 2008.

129. Marcia Myers, David Folkenflik, Albert Sehlstedt Jr., "Henry Knott Sr. dies, philanthropist was 89, construction tycoon gave fortunes to hospitals, schools," *Baltimore Sun*, November 27, 1995. Ivan Penn, "Descendants of Knott caught in web he feared, Estate: A multimillionaire's heirs disagree over the distribution of the family's wealth," *Baltimore Sun*, September 30, 2004. Nicole Fuller,

"Knott battle could be over: Representatives of mother's estate dismissed, but feud continues," *Baltimore Sun*, December 17, 2006.

130. Joel Siegel, "Cold Case: Tom Carvel's Ice Cream Empire Churned Up a Substantial Estate and a Bitter, Dickensian Fight Over His Money. Now a Lawsuit Asks, Was He Murdered?" *Condé Nast Portfolio*, August 2008.

131. Thomas Easton, "Meltdown of an ice cream fortune," *Forbes*, June 15, 1998.

132. Nikila Srinivasan *Silver Linings*, (Mumbai: Better Yourself Books, The Bombay Saint Paul Society, 2007), 112.

133. "How Buffett's Gifts Will Work," *Chronicle of Philanthropy*, July 20, 2006.

134. Ian Wilhelm, "Gates Foundation Announces that It Doesn't Plan to Operate Forever," *Chronicle of Philanthropy*, December 7, 2006.

135. Viktor Frankl, *Man's Search for Meaning* (Boston: Beacon Press, 1959).

136. Milton and Rose D. Friedman, Free to Choose (New York: Harcourt Brace Jovanovich, 1980), 148.

Made in the USA
Middletown, DE
09 June 2023

32335053R00109